Advance Praise for
Inner-City Entrepreneurship Development

"The microcredit revolution has come thundering through the world of economic development. Nitin Bhatt cuts through the hyperbole to explain why approaches that work in Bangladesh and Bolivia are proving so difficult in the United States. With new data and hardheaded thinking, Bhatt takes a fresh look at obstacles and opportunities. While providing rich institutional and financial analyses, Bhatt never loses sight of the ultimate bottom line—how to empower communities and expand opportunities for the poorest working Americans."

—JONATHAN MORDUCH
New York University

"Nitin Bhatt offers readers original analyses of microloan programs in California, results of other studies, Third World experience, and application of the New Institutional Economics. He argues convincingly that successful replication of inspiring Third World microfinance models in the U.S. is unlikely. The causes he cites are the differences in institutional, market, and social contexts and the incentives and opportunities these either create or destroy. A valuable contribution to public policy, this book could save billions for U.S. taxpayers by separating wishful thinking from inner-city reality, and hype from accountability. It is not yet possible to sketch a viable grand design, but Bhatt's conclusions and suggestions help construct the foundation."

—J. D. VON PISCHKE
President, Frontier Finance International

"This important book provides fresh and valuable insights on what works and what doesn't in microcredit programs. With meticulous research, a critical eye, and a clear writer's touch, Nitin Bhatt effectively details both the challenges and opportunities for microlending initiatives to spur entrepreneurship and economic development."

—RAYMOND W. SMILOR
President, Foundation for Enterprise Development

"Even the so-called success stories in the microcredit field, almost all of which are located in rural areas of developing countries, are being found to be somewhat more qualified successes than had previously been thought. Nevertheless, this study of microcredit in California shows that applications that have not taken seriously the importance of the incentive structure derived from program design and sufficiently adjusted for very different environmental conditions are doomed to failure and lack of sustainability. This study by Bhatt goes beyond the negatives, however, to identify a number of design features that could greatly enhance the prospects for success in microcredit and entrepreneurial development even in more difficult urban environments."

—JEFF NUGENT
Department of Economics,
University of Southern California

Inner-City Entrepreneurship Development

Inner-City Entrepreneurship Development

THE MICROCREDIT CHALLENGE

NITIN BHATT

ICS PRESS

INSTITUTE FOR CONTEMPORARY STUDIES
OAKLAND, CALIFORNIA

This book is a publication of the Institute for Contemporary Studies, a nonprofit, nonpartisan public policy research organization. The analyses, conclusions, and opinions expressed in ICS Press publications are those of the authors and not necessarily those of the Institute or its officers, its directors, or others associated with, or funding, its work.

Inquiries, book orders, and catalog requests should be addressed to ICS Press, Latham Square, 1611 Telegraph Avenue, Suite 406, Oakland, CA 94612. Tel.: (510) 238-5010; Fax: (510) 238-8440; Internet: www.icspress.com. For book orders and catalog requests, call toll free in the United States: (800) 326-0263.

0 9 8 7 6 5 4 3 2 1

Library of Congress Cataloging-in-Publication Data

Bhatt, Nitin, 1968–
        Inner-city entrepreneurship development : the microcredit challenge / Nitin Bhatt.
             p. cm.
        Subtitle on p. [1] of cover: the microcredit challenge.
        includes bibliographical references and index.
        ISBN 1-55815-517-1 (pbk.)
        1. Microfinance—California—Los Angeles. 2. Small business—California—Los Angeles. 3. Microfinance. 4. Small business. I. Title.

HG178.33.U6 B48 2001
338.6'42'0979494—dc21
                                                        2001016653

Contents

List of Tables and Figures   vii

A Note from the Publisher   ix

Preface   xi

Chapter 1.   The Microcredit Revolution   1

Chapter 2.   Framework for Program Evaluation   25

Chapter 3.   Rationale   47

Chapter 4.   Loan Repayment Performance   81

Chapter 5.   Sustainability   115

Chapter 6.   Potential   135

Appendix: Data Collection Methodology   159

References   165

Index   181

About the Author   187

About ICS   188

Tables and Figures

Table 2.1	Microenterprise activities in the United States and abroad	36
Table 3.1	Distribution of financial services in Los Angeles by census tract median income	52
Table 3.2	Density of financial services around bank branches closed and opened, 1988–1993	53
Table 3.3	Socioeconomic characteristics of micro-entrepreneurs surveyed in California (discrete variables)	64
Table 3.4	Socioeconomic characteristics of micro-entrepreneurs surveyed in California (continuous variables)	65
Table 3.5	Some determinants of perceived constraints to enterprise development	66
Table 3.6	Some determinants of perceived constraints to capital access	73
Figure 3.1	Perceived constraints to enterprise development	65
Figure 3.2	Perceived constraints to capital access	72
Table 4.1	Definition of individual-level variables for four microcredit programs	93
Table 4.2	Descriptive statistics for four microcredit programs	94

Table 4.3   Logit model of repayment performance for
            four microcredit programs   95
Table 4.4   Repayment performance for NEP
            in California   100
Table 4.5   Definition of independent variables for NEP
            in California   100
Table 4.6   Logit model of repayment performance for
            NEP in California   100
Table 5.1   Portfolio at risk for California-based WDA
            program   126
Table 5.2   Annual loan loss for California-based WDA
            program   126
Table 5.3   Annual interest rates and fee structures for
            189 U.S. microcredit programs   129
Table 5.4   Loan disbursement record for California-
            based WDA program   131

A Note from the Publisher

How do we develop policy and intervene in impoverished communities in such a way as to build social, political, and economic wealth rather than dependency? This is one, if not the key, question of urban policy as it relates to poor inner-city neighborhoods.

Over the past 20 years a number of practitioners and scholars have focused on building asset-based policies. At the core of these policies is an effort to overcome institutional poverty, that is, to provide inner cities with the institutions and tools that will allow them to build their capacities and make their communities self-organizing—if not self-governing.

One of these capacity-building efforts has been the microcredit-microenterprise movement. The theory is straightforward. Some percentage of poverty is caused by potential entrepreneurs' lack of access to capital. An empirical linchpin for this theory is found in the experiences of Bangladesh's Grameen Bank and in the success of Latin America's ACCION International in lending small amounts of money to poor women.

In the late 1980s a number of American foundations and government agencies became interested in translating the foreign microlending experience to the United States. Microlending had a strong appeal for both the right and the left. For the right, it would bring capitalism to our inner cities. For the left, it would bring participation, social empowerment, and some equity in financing, getting the country beyond big lending institutions.

As Nitin Bhatt demonstrates in this powerful book, the translation of a working idea from abroad to the United States has been neither direct nor smooth. What this book does through a review of past experience and new research is to transform a supposed panacea into a working tool that can be used effectively when designed to meet local conditions and institutions.

For the academic, the author's treatment of the critical role that trust and reciprocity play in building going concerns will strike home as a true and critical base for institution building. Policy makers and practitioners trying to design programs will find the author's ideas on building effective loan programs useful to their work.

As with all new program efforts, time to work out flaws is a critical component of a commitment to success. Microcredit and microenterprises still have an important role to play in overcoming institutional poverty in our inner cities. This book provides policy and grant makers with information critical to realizing that goal.

—ROBERT B. HAWKINS, JR.
President and CEO,
Institute for Contemporary Studies

Preface

The idea for this book came out of my research and consulting work in entrepreneurship and economic development in the 1990s.

As a researcher, I was concerned about one of the most significant challenges facing American policy makers: the state of its inner cities. Decades of government investments in development projects had resulted in few tangible economic benefits for inner-city residents, leading some policy makers to promote an increasingly popular Third World development strategy—microlending—to spur grassroots entrepreneurship and create economic opportunities in the inner city. To implement the strategy, nonprofits, community-based organizations, and often government entities were selected as intermediaries to provide loans, and often training and technical assistance, to prospective and existing small-business owners. Equipped with capital and business knowledge, these entrepreneurs were expected to successfully engage in self-employment, increase their incomes and assets, and, over time, become self-sufficient and productive citizens. During the 1990s, the popular press made a strong case for widespread replication of microcredit institutions across the United States, and public and private sector investment in such programs grew exponentially.

As a management consultant, I had the opportunity to interact with nonprofit and finance professionals involved with the implementation of such programs. Informal discussions and anecdotal evidence provided by them (and a few leading academics) suggested major challenges to replicating Third World microcredit models in U.S. inner cities, and raised questions about the reportedly superior performance and impact of such initiatives. These conversations and reports led to some fundamental questions: What kinds of operational challenges do microcredit institutions face in the United States? What is their loan repayment performance? What factors impact their operational and financial viability? To what extent can microcredit models work in the United States?

This book addresses these critical questions by analyzing the performance of microcredit programs in California as well as other existing studies and consulting reports on the performance of microfinance institutions in the United States and abroad. Its conclusions, however, extend beyond an analysis of organizational performance. They refer also to important public policy issues that relate to the operation of development finance institutions, such as the provision of public subsidies and governance of donor-funded nonprofit organizations.

I offer this book in the hope that it will help those interested in this field—bankers, nonprofit managers, foundation personnel, and policy makers—to understand better the systemic roots of the problems that confront microfinance institutions. This may lead to new and more effective strategies and vehicles for supporting and nurturing inner-city entrepreneurship.

This book could not have been written without the support and assistance I received from many people. My deepest appreciation goes to Shui-Yan Tang, who served as my mentor and research partner. I thank him for allowing me to liberally use in this book ideas that we developed together. I also profited from comments by J. D. Von Pischke, Mark Schreiner, Timothy Bates, Jonathan Morduch, Gerald Caiden, Jeffrey Nugent, Gary Painter, and Alex Counts, and would like to thank these individuals for taking the time to read and help improve the various versions of my manuscript. Throughout work on this book I sought out microfinance and economic development experts, benefiting greatly from discussions, some brief and some long, with them. These stimulating individuals include Mari Riddle, Saundra Knox, Villa Mills, D. A. Tran, Bill Burrus, Jack Litzenberg, and the board members, managers, and staff of the institutions that participated in this research study. I thank them all for their help in shaping my thoughts and analyses. Needless to say, any remaining faults are solely mine and should not be ascribed to the persons whose assistance is acknowledged above.

Financial support for this research was provided by Ewing Marion Kauffman Foundation's Center for Entrepreneurial Leadership, and I thank Raymond Smilor and Judith Cone for their help in sponsoring this study. University of Southern California's Center for International Business Education and Research (CIBEAR) supported my trip to the Grameen Bank in Bangladesh, where I benefited from discussions with bank staff and customers. I would also like to thank Robert B. Hawkins, Jr., of the Institute for Contemporary Studies, for encouraging me to prepare the manuscript for publication. Editorial and technical support from Perenna Fleming and Melissa Stein is also gratefully acknowledged. And last, but not least, I would like to thank my entire family: my parents Bimal and Dinesh, my sister Mamta and brother-in-law Alok, my parents-in-law Hema and Prafulla, and my wife, Rashmi, for their love and patient support as I completed this book.

This book is dedicated to the millions of men and women around the world who are engaged in self-employment. Despite the challenges that come with starting and running one's own venture, most of these individuals demonstrate a remarkable determination to design their own destiny and succeed in the face of all odds. Indeed, it is their unwavering entrepreneurial spirit that has strengthened my commitment to entrepreneurship and economic development.

CHAPTER ONE

The Microcredit Revolution

Among the various strategies suggested for the development of inner-city communities across the United States, microentrepreneurship has received considerable attention in recent years. It is argued that the microenterprise sector not only increases the flow of goods and services in neglected neighborhoods but often provides income and asset-enhancing opportunities for its residents. As a result, scholars and policy makers are increasingly stressing the importance of microenterprises in alleviating poverty and spurring community economic development (Balkin, 1989a&b; Else and Raheim, 1992; Friedman et al., 1995; Clark and Kays, 1999; Raheim and Alter, 1998).

Loosely defined as businesses with fewer than five employees and credit requirements of $500 to $25,000,[1] many of these small-scale enterprises[2] are launched by low-income individuals,[3] are generally owner-operated, are more labor- than capital-intensive, have high relative production costs, and usually lack technical expertise in business operations and management. Some observers have suggested that the establishment of such businesses should be encouraged because "unlike the wide range of government-sponsored welfare programs that seem to contribute to the dependency and despair of the underclass, microenterprises can potentially break the cycle of dependency and hopelessness by restoring initiative, responsibility, and dignity" (Solomon, 1992, p. 1).

It is often argued that the microenterprise sector's potential for further growth has been constrained by one major factor—its limited access to business credit (Davis, 1995; Drier, 1991; Drury et al., 1994; Grzywinski et al., 1992; Nelson, 1994; Raheim, 1997; Soloman, 1992). Those who want to start or expand microbusinesses find it extremely difficult to obtain loans from a banking system oriented in favor of lending to large enterprises (Barringer, 1993; Dymski, 1996; Giles, 1993; Light and Pham, 1998; Yinger, 1998). Traditional banks are reluctant to make loans to such entrepreneurs for a number of reasons.

First, given the lack of proper record keeping it is extremely difficult to assess the creditworthiness of loan applicants and their enterprises. Such assessments are also made difficult by the unavailability of data on the potential of the markets within which microentrepreneurs operate. Other related difficulties may include applicants' lack of a track record in entrepreneurship, insufficient cash flow, high debt-to-income ratio, a poor credit record, and lack of collateral. Second, the administrative costs of booking and servicing small loans are very high. When combined with the small amount of interest income generated from such credits, banks end up making little or no profit on small loans.[4] As a result of the high risks and administrative costs involved in microlending, credit markets often "fail" small-scale entrepreneurs by refusing them loans.[5]

MICROCREDIT PROGRAMS
IN THE THIRD WORLD

Recognizing this problem, some nongovernmental organizations and public-private partnerships have spearheaded a quiet revolution that seeks to change the fate of these entrepreneurs. Encouraged by the success of such internationally recognized microlending "models" as Bangladesh's Grameen Bank and Latin America's ACCION International in spurring grassroots entrepreneurship, a number of policy makers and donors have advocated support for implementing similar initiatives in the United States (Auwal, 1996; Solomon, 1992).

The accomplishments of these overseas initiatives are indeed noteworthy. The Grameen Bank, which started as a pilot project in 1976 with the disbursement of a total of $27 in loans to 42 poor microentrepreneurs to help them purchase bamboo, has grown into an economic development giant, having disbursed more than $2.9 billion in credit to 2.4 million poor borrowers.[6] The bank disburses up to $40 million in loans per month to a clientele that is 94 percent female. Most loans are for one year, the average loan balance is $134, and repayments are weekly. ACCION International's Latin American operations have also been effective in financing small-scale entrepreneurs, having lent over $2.2 billion since 1973.[7] Thirteen of their 21 affiliate programs are operationally self-sufficient, while eight are financially self-sufficient.[8] ACCION's most well known program, BancoSol, has a largely urban and nonpoor clientele (Morduch, 1999; Navajas et al., 2000). Average loan balances are $909 and loan terms are generally 4 to 12 months, with flexible weekly or biweekly repayments. The bank reports return on assets of 4.5 percent—a figure that surpasses the performance of most conventional commercial banks. Such superior performance has prompted the development community to attempt to replicate the above programs and to provide financing to entrepreneurs in low-income communities by extending loans ranging from a few hundred to several thousand dollars.

One innovative method adopted by these microcredit agencies is group-based lending (Barenbach and Guzman, 1994).[9] In such programs, prospective borrowers are made to organize themselves to form groups of four to seven members and provide a mutual guarantee for loan repayment. Although no collateral or credit checks are required for loan approval, the group formation process involves intensive due diligence to ensure that only those who are able and willing to handle debt actually get to participate. In some programs, the loan is made not to the individual but to the group, which then makes the capital available to one or more group members. In other models, the loan is made to one group member, and others in the group become eligible for the loan, on a rotating basis, once the initial borrower proves her creditworthiness by making payments on time. Each member within the group is thus individually and collectively responsible for the credit rating of the group and for ensuring that the funding cycle is not broken because of a default in the payment schedule.[10]

Despite high rates of interest on the loans,[11] repayment rates in successful overseas programs that employ such models of unsecured and joint-liability lending have been very high, averaging between 92 and 97 percent.[12] This is especially impressive given that state-supported development banks in most Third World countries have rarely recovered over 75 percent of loans disbursed.[13] Indeed, it is largely the risk reduction feature of group-based lending that has attracted the attention of researchers around the world (Bhatt and Tang, 1998 a&b; Besley and Coate, 1995; Devereux and Fishe, 1993; Huppi and Feder, 1990; Stiglitz, 1990; Varian, 1990). Yet it is not the theoretical soundness of Third World microcredit models but rather their intuitive appeal among a variety of development practitioners that has led to widespread support worldwide.[14]

First, microcredit programs appeal to the "participatory and people centered development" lobby because microcredit initiatives, such as group lending and village banking programs in some Third World countries, "include" entrepreneurs in the design, implementation, and evaluation of the programs—participation that is considered key to building sustainable development capacity (Korten, 1990; World Bank, 1996). Second, such programs appeal to activists of the "women in development" lobby. Some observers believe that empowering women and addressing gender discrimination are key to the long-term development of children, families, and communities but have long been sidelined in the design of development projects (Male, 1993; Rodriguez, 1995).

Third, some development experts, including advocates of the above two lobbies, promote microcredit programs as part of the "poverty alleviation" lobby. Some scholars, for example, argue that microcredit can help increase the economic self-sufficiency of the poor (Hulme and Mosely, 1996; Khandker, 1996). Others suggest that it can reduce their vulnerability to income shocks by allowing them to put their otherwise idle labor into productive use (Morduch, 1999). Finally, microcredit programs also seem to receive some support by the "economic growth" lobby. Some observers, for instance, proclaim that in the presence of an enabling economic environment, microenterprises can serve as a seedbed of industrialization and lead to economic growth in the long run (Grosh and Somolekae, 1996).

Given the strong support from many different fronts, the last 15 years have witnessed an intensified push for establishing microcredit programs in the United States, often celebrated by the popular press as the transfer of technology from the Third World to the First. Stark similarities in problems of developing countries and U.S. inner cities have been cited, and Third World solutions for solving America's problems of poverty and jobless-ness have been recommended. According to Jordan (1993), for example,

> The deplorable condition of a lot of our neighborhoods in major cities across this country is clear evidence that some-thing is terribly wrong . . . the situation [is] as if we have a third-world nation existing within our own borders. So it is useful, I think, to reflect on what we have learned from developing countries about the role of credit and economic development. (p. 1)

MICROCREDIT PROGRAMS IN THE UNITED STATES

Eager to learn from and replicate the experiences of a handful of prominent Third World lending programs, policy makers and donors in the United States have launched a number of initiatives.[15] In 1988 the Ford Foundation funded a "technology transfer" project, whose objective was "to stimulate reciprocal advisory services between development banking practitioners (from Bangladesh to North America) to strengthen the develop-ment of the group-based lending methodology as a strategy for poverty alleviation" (Nelson, 1994, p. xi). Although most such efforts initially focused on group lending techniques and recommended targeting the poorest of the poor, such an approach has since expanded to include individual lending and nonpoor entrepreneurs.

Early group-based microcredit programs—such as the Full Circle Fund of the Women's Self Employment Project, launched in 1986 in Chicago, and the Good Faith Fund, launched in 1988

in Pine Bluff, Arkansas—initially targeted informal sector entrepreneurs and individuals receiving public assistance. Since
self-employment was increasingly being promoted as a possible
welfare-to-work strategy, several programs around the country
followed suit. Prominent examples included the federally supported Neighborhood Enterprise Centers, launched in 1989 by
the Neighborhood Reinvestment Corporation, and the Refugee
Microenterprise Programs, launched in 1990 by the Department of
Health and Human Services' Office of Refugee Resettlement. In
keeping with their charge of alleviating poverty by promoting self-
employment, these initiatives provided a range of inputs for their
clients, including entrepreneurship training, business assistance,
and even health and human services.

As the microcredit industry matured in the 1990s, a "second
wave" of initiatives evolved that adopted a mix of enterprise
development techniques. In addition to assisting poor entrepreneurs, programs began targeting established microentrepreneurs
with higher levels of assets, incomes, and education. Two prominent programs that fall within this category are the affiliates
of the Working Capital program, with operations in New
Hampshire, Maine, Vermont, Massachusetts, Florida, and
Delaware, and the U.S. network of ACCION International, with
sites in New York, Texas, California, New Mexico, and Illinois.[16]

It is estimated that microcredit programs in the two "waves"
have disbursed over $160 million in financing to small-scale entre-
preneurs. Currently, these programs serve a variety of clients,
including moderate-income individuals, the working poor, the
unemployed, and those on welfare. In 1997, nearly 200 microcredit initiatives that were capitalized with over $129 million
disbursed $33,262,529 to 6,153 borrowers, with an average loan
size of $5,406. Sixty-two percent of the programs also provided
training and technical assistance to build the human capital of
prospective and existing entrepreneurs (Aspen Institute, 1999).

Supporters argue that these financial and nonfinancial services can result in significant economic and social benefits for
program participants. For example, a number of microcredit programs extend capital to presumably otherwise credit-constrained
individuals—entrepreneurs who are engaged in a wide variety of
small-scale retailing, wholesaling, and manufacturing activities,
including operating gift shops, apparel production businesses,
desktop publishing companies, and grocery and jewelry outlets
at swap meets. Some low-income women use self-employment
as part of an income-patching strategy, combining entrepreneurial profits with wage earnings to enhance their financial
self-sufficiency. Access to credit, it is thought, can enable such
microentrepreneurs to maintain a sufficient supply of capital to
purchase supplies and inventory, invest in assets such as tools and
equipment, maintain or expand operations, and in some cases,
even generate employment opportunities.

Others highlight the social benefits of microcredit initiatives
(Solomon, 1992). The training and networking opportunities
provided by many programs build a sense of community in low-
income neighborhoods. For instance, borrowers in a number of
programs act as each other's financial advisors and help peers
make decisions in both business and personal contexts. Program
participants often form informal associations for making contacts
and referrals, leveraging each other's knowledge and skills, and
venturing with a collaborative spirit. Many observers believe
that for individuals who face such challenges as poverty, language
barriers, inadequate skills, and insufficient education, this spirit
of reciprocity can go a long way in building social capital that is
vital for both individual and community empowerment.

It is perhaps this potential of microenterprise development
programs to positively impact both economic development and
social welfare that accounts for their popularity in development
circles. Many scholars and policy makers have recommended

widespread replication of such programs across the country, arguing that the social benefits of these programs exceed their social costs (Benus et al., 1995; Friedman et al., 1995; Raheim, 1997).[17] As a result, microenterprise initiatives have grown from less than 10 in 1987 to over 280 in 1997.[18]

MIXED RESULTS

While microcredit is viewed by many as a Third World development tool that has immense potential in the United States, the performance of microcredit programs over the last 15 years has been decidedly mixed. While some studies suggest that "microcredit" has had a positive economic impact on microentrepreneurs, others suggest that many "microcredit programs" are operationally and financially unsustainable.

Three prominent research studies suggest that effectively run microcredit programs have positive impacts on individuals and communities. These investigations are especially instructive since they evaluate impacts on three different types of populations: largely poor, a mix of poor and nonpoor, and largely nonpoor. The first study documents the results of the Self-employment Demonstration Project, a national project implemented by the Corporation for Enterprise Development in Iowa, Maryland, Michigan, Minnesota, and Mississippi (Raheim, 1997). The program provided group business training, personal development workshops, individual technical assistance, and financing services to 1,300 individuals on public assistance, 408 of whom started businesses during the demonstration. Seventy-nine percent of the businesses started by welfare recipients were still in operation 2.6 years after being launched, creating about 1.5 jobs each and increasing each entrepreneur's gross personal assets by about $8,750.

The second investigation is Aspen Institute's longitudinal study of 405 poor and nonpoor microentrepreneurs. The study tracked the progress of these individuals from 1991 to 1997 (Clark and Kays, 1999). Seventy-two percent of the 133 poor microentrepreneurs in the study experienced average income gains of $8,484 over five years, allowing 53 percent of them to move out of poverty and to reduce their reliance on government assistance by 61 percent. The survival rate of the businesses was 49 percent after five years—comparable to ventures with similar characteristics and owners. Perhaps most importantly, for those who were still in business after five years, their businesses had been a major contributor to increases in household income— accounting for 37 percent of such increases.

A third study of 848 largely nonpoor microentrepreneurs who participated in six ACCION programs also reveals positive client benefits (Himes with Servon, 1998). Over an average of 17 months, clients with three loans increased their average monthly profits by 47 percent, business equity by 42 percent, and take-home income by 38 percent. Although the study suggests that microcredit did not directly lead to job creation, its contribution to the financial growth of microentrepreneurs was significant. For example, low-income clients who received four loans from an ACCION program increased their business profits by 96 percent, to an average of $500 a month, and their business equity by 46 percent, to an average of nearly $6,000.

Despite the positive client impacts reported in these studies, Schreiner (1999c) cautions against the tendency of microcredit proponents to overstate its potential in helping the poor. In particular, he argues that most evaluations done on microcredit programs in the United States, as is the case in the three studies mentioned earlier, lack comparisons with control groups. Absent such controls, it is difficult to determine whether the microloan itself, or some other nonprogrammatic factor, was actually responsible for the improvement in the client's economic conditions.

The validity of some of these studies was further put in doubt as scholars began to look more closely at how performance data were reported. For example, Servon and Bates (1998, p. 422) pointed out that when Raheim (1996, p. 72) reported a mean income of $21,231 for his sample of microcredit recipients, the number actually referred to the microenterprise's gross sales rather than profits. According to Servon and Bates's own calculation, the net profit for the average microenterprise was only $3,011.

Even though the "message" of microcredit may have had positive impacts, many of its "messengers"—the microcredit programs—have been less successful. Specifically, research suggests that with a few exceptions,[19] most U.S. programs are faced with critical challenges, including the lack of outreach and sustainability (Bates, 1997; Bhatt et al., 1999b; Buntin, 1997; Bates and Servon, 1996; Schreiner, 1999d; Servon, 1999). For example, Bhatt et al.'s (1999a) survey of loan programs in California revealed that each program made only seven loans per year on average, and that more than half of the capital available for lending sat idle. Some program managers attributed the low volume of loans to a lack of viable proposals from people who would be likely to repay the money; others reported a lack of demand. Further, programs suffered from high loan losses and excessive overhead costs, and thus had to depend on external subsidies to stay in business.

Despite such external support, however, many programs did not survive beyond the short run. For instance, nearly 30 percent of the microcredit programs that operated in California in 1996 had been shut down by 1998, reminding us of the prediction made by Adams and Von Pischke (1992), who warned that efforts to replicate the *very few* successful Third World programs would lead to the failure of many microcredit initiatives, especially when the development community adopts a "relatively successful model without a grasp of the substance that animates and sustains it" (p. 1468). The lack of viability at both the entrepreneur and program levels also strikes a chord with Bates's (1995) observation regarding the general futility of using microcredit as an economic development tool for inner-city revitalization.

> From the late 1960s to the mid-1980s the Economic Opportunity Loan (EOL) program, administered by the Small Business Administration, provided more loans to minority businesses than all other federal-government programs combined. The median loan size was less than $10,000, and loan recipients commonly ran small retail operations in inner-city minority communities. The default rate among borrowers starting new businesses exceeded 70%. Of those who were repaying their loans, many eventually closed down because of their inability to make a decent living running tiny businesses in the ghetto. The EOL program, its credibility destroyed by massive ineffectiveness, was terminated in 1984; yet its clones continue to be widespread in the 1990s at all levels of government and in the nonprofit sector as well. (p. 27)

Despite the above warnings, however, policy makers, program designers, and practitioners have knowingly, and sometimes unknowingly, formulated and implemented Third World microcredit models in U.S. inner cities without adequate attention to design features that are critical to making such programs viable.

KEYS TO PROGRAM VIABILITY

Any organization seeking to provide microcredit to entrepreneurs needs to be concerned about its ability to stay in business beyond the short term. Since the viability of a microcredit program depends to a large extent on the stability of its client base, it is critical for programs to serve entrepreneurs who are both able and willing to repay the loans. In addition, the costs and risks associated with loan delivery techniques, financial products, nonfinancial services, management practices, and governance structures impact a program's ability to stay in business. Given these factors, three particular problems must be addressed in developing viable microcredit programs: first, how to design a program that ensures that clients will be *able* to repay the loans; second, how to make certain that borrowers, in addition to being able, will also be *willing* to fulfill their financial obligations; third, how to ensure the *operational sustainability* of programs as they serve microentrepreneurs.

Each of these problems needs to be tackled by adopting different yet related strategies. The ability problem requires an analysis of the debt capacity of individuals (adequate debt capacity implies that the combination of cash generated from clients' businesses and household incomes is both adequate *and* available to make timely loan repayments) and an assessment of the capital and noncapital constraints on enterprise development. The provision of credit and general business training are often ineffective for many poor individuals seeking to generate income and earn some extra money in the short run. This is because, unlike in the Third World, microentrepreneurs in the United States often face low levels of revenues and profits due to high input costs, weak market demand, and low-cost competing products and services, often available through more established players in the market. For the most part, it is an unfavorable market environment that poses a major challenge to microentrepreneurs and, by extension, to the viability of microcredit programs.

The willingness problem can be addressed by isolating design features that create value for entrepreneurs and motivate them to establish long-term relationships with lending agencies. For example, it is often thought that peer pressure and support account for the superior portfolio performance of successful Third World programs. While high reserves of social capital surely play an important role in ensuring repayment, equally critical is the high dependency of borrowers on future loans. Since virtually all successful overseas programs charge interest rates that are less than those charged by moneylenders, and since programs craft financial products and service-delivery strategies that are client-tailored, convenient, and stable, individuals are happy with the quality of services and motivated to maintain an ongoing relationship with the lender. In other words, they are willing to do what it takes to repay the loans and maintain a good credit standing. But many people in the United States are not dependent on the microcredit programs for future access to credit. In some instances, this low dependency is the result of access to alternative sources of capital, including income from wage employment. In other cases, individuals perceive the costs of accessing loans as exceeding the benefits due to the high transaction costs[20] incurred, and as a result, they do not see much value in maintaining an ongoing relationship with the programs. Lenders would do well to thoroughly understand their target market's characteristics, preferences, and constraints, and to then design products and services that motivate borrowers to maintain long-term relationships with them.

The operational sustainability challenge can be confronted by addressing critical issues related to financial, social, and administrative intermediation. As chapters 3, 4, and 5 will demonstrate, while the first two intermediation challenges can be confronted by addressing the ability and willingness problems at a program-management level, the third requires the attention of a program's leadership, board, and sponsoring agencies. This is because problems in administrative intermediation arise due to challenges associated with fiscal instability and program governance. To address the former, a focus on enhancing sustainability needs to be fundamental to an organization's strategic planning process. Programs that do not move toward making operational self-sufficiency a priority remain dependent on subsidies to keep their doors open. Although subsidies are not "bad" per se,[21] evidence from U.S. microcredit programs suggests that once the external funding dries up, organizations fold, as do sources of financing for the community. To boost operational sustainability, programs must charge interest rates and fees, within legal bounds, that are appropriate given the levels of risk they assume. Further, to increase earned income, programs may consider adopting a multiproduct strategy and making larger loans (greater than $25,000) that can cross-subsidize the "losses" incurred in making smaller loans.

To confront the governance problem, the development community must recognize that the likelihood of operational inefficiencies increases when various stakeholders—borrowers, field staff, program managers, boards of directors, and fiscal sponsors—face incompatible incentives. For example, managers often find themselves unable to articulate a coherent set of goals and objectives when programs secure funding from multiple sponsors who want to serve different target markets and have different criteria for assessing client eligibility and program outcomes. For example, while some sponsors require programs to serve low-moderate income women and minorities, others focus on poor immigrants and refugee communities. While some assess program performance by changes in the incomes and assets of participants, others are concerned with the ability of participants to create employment opportunities. In order to align stakeholder incentives, it is therefore critical for sponsors not only to invest resources in building appropriate outreach and management capacity but also to establish common "industry standards" that can be consistently employed for evaluating performance and making funding decisions.

RESEARCH METHODOLOGY

This research employs a mix of qualitative and quantitative techniques using data obtained from multiple sources. We examine existing studies of microcredit programs in the United States and overseas, assess the enterprise development constraints of a cross section of microentrepreneurs, and analyze the records of several of the early microcredit replications to isolate features that are likely to enhance the viability of microcredit programs in the United States.

Given the relatively longer history of microcredit programs overseas, a number of scholars have analyzed a host of theoretical and policy puzzles as they relate to the Third World context. This vast literature provided us with valuable information and background on various aspects of program design and implementation. Since an understanding of the contextual similarities and differences between the Third World and the United States is key to policy formulation, we identified "practices" that seemed to impact performance across a wide variety of socioeconomic environments and, therefore, could be potentially useful for informing program design in the United States. Further, we surveyed microentrepreneurs who had been declined bank loans and had approached three microenterprise development programs for assistance. Upon assessing the financial and nonfinancial barriers they faced in developing microbusinesses, and analyzing how those challenges were related to their socioeconomic characteristics, we conducted focus group interviews to develop a deeper understanding of the constraints reported in the surveys. Finally, we studied four of the oldest microcredit programs in California to analyze factors associated with loan repayment performance and program sustainability. Information on borrower characteristics and experiences was obtained in part from agency archives, from a survey and interviews with the borrowers of one of the programs, and from focus group sessions and interviews with the loan officers, managers, and board members of these organizations. The following programs were selected for the study:[22]

Community Enterprise Program assists disadvantaged refugees in attaining economic self-sufficiency through various microenterprise development services that include group-based lending and training programs. The agency has been disbursing credit to groups since 1991. Its primary target market is Asian and Armenian individuals on public assistance and it is funded mainly by government contracts.

Enterprise Development Corporation has been providing business development services since 1985 to low-moderate income individuals interested in microenterprise development. Training and technical assistance are provided to individuals and groups in such areas as bookkeeping, financial management, sales and marketing, and capital sourcing. Its primary target market is low-moderate income African American and Caucasian entrepreneurs and it is funded by government contracts and foundation grants.

First Chance is dedicated to increasing long-term income and employment opportunities among the marginally self-employed by providing access to credit based on both individual- and group-lending methodologies. Since its inception in 1990, its primary target market is low-moderate income Latino entrepreneurs, primarily women. It is funded by foundation grants, corporate donations, and program income.

Neighborhood Entrepreneurship Program is part of a larger private, nonprofit community-based corporation. The organization was one of the four group-based microcredit development pilot programs launched nationwide in 1989 by the congressionally chartered Neighborhood Reinvestment Corporation, whose objective was to encourage entrepreneurial activity among disadvantaged populations, especially minorities and women. It provides loans and training to its clients who are mostly low-income African American and Caucasian women entrepreneurs. It is funded primarily by government contracts.

Women's Development Association was founded in 1989 for providing assistance to low-income individuals, primarily women, in achieving economic self-sufficiency through self-employment. Although WDA ceased operation in 1996, its former executive director made available to us agency and borrower data from the organization's archives. It provided loans, training, and technical assistance to both individual and group borrowers, and its client base consisted primarily of African Americans and Latinos. It was funded by various government contracts and foundation grants.

These agencies provided us with a rich diversity of experiences in microenterprise development. Not only did they serve different ethnic groups, including Asians, African Americans, Latinos, and Caucasians, they also targeted individuals belonging to different economic backgrounds, from those on public assistance to those who were not "poor" but had low-moderate level incomes. In addition, the programs' services ranged from only lending to the provision of training and technical assistance as well. Finally, all five programs had different funding sources, ranging from government contracts and foundation grants to corporate donations and program incomes.

PLAN OF THE BOOK

The plan for the rest of the book is as follows. Chapter 2 develops a framework for evaluating the viability of microcredit programs. Chapter 3 assesses the barriers faced by entrepreneurs in developing small-scale enterprises. Chapter 4 analyzes the determinants of loan repayment performance. Chapter 5 investigates the limited sustainability of programs in the United States. Chapter 6 presents a framework for building the capacity of microcredit initiatives. It concludes that transforming the microcredit promise[23] into cost-effective policies and viable programs that can enhance the welfare of microentrepreneurs in the United States is a complex proposition. It requires policy makers, practitioners, and donors to focus not simply on replicating successful models but on building sustainable organizations, keeping in mind the implications of a region's socioeconomic and institutional characteristics on program performance. Absent such a focus, microcredit programs, like many other development initiatives in the past, are unlikely to bear fruit.

NOTES

1. In general, microenterprise finance is characterized by small loans relative to GDP. "The local financial market is a reference point . . . because microfinance reaches clients who have not had access to formal financial markets. . . . For example, where commercial bankers do not make loans of less than $1,000, the upper bound of a microloan could be defined as $1,000. . . ." (Von Pischke, 1999, p. 1).

2. The words *microenterprises* and *small-scale enterprises,* and *microentrepreneurs* and *small-scale entrepreneurs,* are used interchangeably throughout the book.

3. The U.S. Department of Housing and Urban Development defines "low-income" people as individuals earning less than 80 percent of the median income of a certain area. In the context of microenterprise development programs, however, *low-income* generally refers to the poverty status of an individual. Different federal agencies, community economic development supporters, and microenterprise development practitioners employ different operational definitions of "poor."

For example, according to the U.S. Department of Health and Human Services, the federal poverty line is calculated in terms of the income it takes to feed a family based on the number of family members. In 1999, for instance, this stood at $16,700 for a family of four. Many microenterprise researchers choose to use a percentage multiple of the above guideline. Clark and Kays (1999), for instance, boost the poverty threshold to 150 percent in classifying individuals in low-income and non–low-income groups. Some practitioners argue that microenterprise programs ought to focus not just on low-income people but also on moderate-income individuals, since this target group may also need financial assistance to support their self-employment efforts.

4. In developing countries, the "most efficient providers' annual administrative costs and bad debt losses are usually around 20% of the average amount of loans outstanding on their books. A few providers have lower costs, but many microlenders' annual costs are much higher than 20% of the average size of their portfolio" (Von Pischke, 1999, p. 1).

5. Sometimes noneconomic factors may also come into play. According to Grzywinski et al. (1992), for example, "local bankers are unlikely to make loans which threaten to change the local political order. There is a substantial body of evidence that suggests that some bankers in rural areas own their banks for reasons other than maximization of profits. Social standing and political power also often seem to figure in their calculations" (p. 77). In addition, empirical evidence suggests that bankers in urban areas discriminate against loan applicants from minority communities. For a formal analysis of discrimination in urban credit markets, see Dymski (1993).

6. Personal communication, Grameen Bank, February 16, 2000. A good account of Grameen Bank's history and operating philosophy is provided in Counts (1996).

7. Personal communication, ACCION International, February 14, 2000.

8. Programs are operationally self-sufficient when interest and fee income at least cover administrative costs (including noncash expenses such as depreciation and loan loss provisions) and financially self-sufficient when interest and fee income cover all costs, including those of administration, capital, and inflation.

9. Other techniques include lending through credit unions, village banks, and commercial banks. For discussions of these innovations and specific case studies, see Otero and Rhyne (1994).

10. In the case of the Grameen Bank, the sanction for having a group member default is not lack of access to new loans but lack of access to larger loans and new loan products.

11. Effective interest rates on microloans in most prominent Third World programs are anywhere between 20 and 50 percent.

12. It is important to note that comparing repayment rates across programs is meaningless unless loan repayments are measured in a standardized fashion. For example, calculating loan repayment as cumulative amounts received divided by cumulative amounts due is different from computing loan repayment as amount received that was due during a period divided by amount which fell due.

13. "In an extreme example, during the 1980s, one Latin American rural financial institution with more than 500 branches and 27,000 employees received $10.3 billion in fiscal and quasi-fiscal transfers (that is, capital injections and interest subsidies), while recovering only 10–15 percent on its portfolio and serving only 2 percent of the rural population" (Yaron et al., 1998, p. 148). For other examples of challenges associated with development banking, see Adams et al. (1984) and Bhatt and Thorat (2001).

14. It is estimated that there are between 7,000 and 10,000 specialized microlenders worldwide. These institutions probably serve about 15 million clients. The Washington, D.C.–based Microcredit Summit seeks to widen the outreach of microcredit to 100 million of the world's poorest families by 2005, and plans to raise $20 billion for this cause.

15. While microcredit programs have a relatively short history, community development lending in America dates back to the 1960s and 1970s (the "War on Poverty" era) when a number of Community Development Corporations (CDCs) and Community Development Loan Funds (CDLFs) were established to extend credit to individuals who were denied access to traditional capital markets. More recently, capital inputs for entrepreneurs have been extended by the U.S. Department of Commerce's Economic Development Administration (EDA) through the creation of local revolving loan funds (RLFs). But research suggests that

these federal efforts to promote economic development have not been effective, with most agencies reluctant to lend money "despite the existence of long-standing problems such as distressed neighborhoods" (NAPA, 1996, p. 25).

Similarly, neighborhood-based economic development strategies, such as community development banks, have had mixed results. The Los Angeles Community Development Bank, capitalized in 1996 with $435 million and touted as the single largest economic development initiative in the country, had lost a third of the $97 million in loans it had extended as of Sept. 30, 1999 (*New York Times*, 1999). It was designated to serve a 19-square-mile economically depressed area in Los Angeles County.

One of the more successful of such community banking efforts has been the South Shore Bank in Chicago, an initiative that is often suggested as a model for "socially conscious" economic development. Another prominent economic development program that focuses on entrepreneurial approaches to community development is the Local Initiatives Support Corporation (LISC), which is funded by the Ford and MacArthur Foundations. But as argued by Chami and Fischer (1995), these successes in economic development are exceptions.

For a history of community development lending in the United States, see Gunn and Gunn (1991) and Berman and Jurie (1998). For a review of federally sponsored microcredit initiatives, see Raheim et al. (1996) and Servon (1999).

16. These programs are often labeled as "minimalist" initiatives. Unlike "integrated" microcredit programs that also provide training and technical assistance to borrowers, minimalist programs, usually in pursuit of attaining self-sufficiency, choose not to provide such noncredit services. For controversies regarding minimalist versus integrated lending approaches, see Bhatt (1997) and Johnson (1998).

17. See Schreiner (1999a) for a discussion of cost-benefit analyses of microcredit programs.

18. In addition, there are about 80 microenterprise support agencies around the country, including public and private funders, training, consulting and research organizations, and regional and national trade associations (Aspen Institute, 1999).

19. Some noteworthy exceptions include ACCION San Antonio, which is estimated to be 70 percent operationally self-sustainable, and Working Capital Florida, with nearly 1,000 active borrowers.

20. Transaction costs in credit delivery can be conceptualized as non-financial costs incurred by borrowers and lenders during pre-loan disbursement, loan disbursement, and post-loan disbursement activities (Bhatt and Tang, 1998a&b). For borrowers, these may include costs associated with screening potential group members, group formation, agreeing on formal or informal group rules, negotiating with the lender, filling out the necessary paperwork, attending group meetings, and appraising and monitoring each others' projects. For lenders these may include costs associated with searching for loanable funds, designing credit contracts, engaging in community outreach, screening borrowers, assessing project feasibility, evaluating loan applications, providing credit training to staff and borrowers, and monitoring and enforcing loan contracts.

21. See Morduch (1999) and Woller et al. (1999) for a discussion of why subsidies and sustainability are not necessarily incompatible. Some observers argue that Grameen Bank provides an example of why subsidies are not necessarily undesirable. For example, Khandker (1998) argues that Grameen Bank's subsidies yield benefits that exceed the welfare gains associated with other similar development programs. Similarly, Schreiner (1999b), who measures the program's outputs rather than social benefits, concludes that the Grameen Bank seems to be a cost-effective social investment.

22. Names of study institutions have been altered as per our agreement with the participating programs. Absent this arrangement, none of the programs was willing to share its data with us.

23. We owe this term to Morduch (1999).

CHAPTER TWO

Framework for Program Evaluation

The lack of consensus among observers regarding what makes microcredit initiatives successful and how success should be evaluated, complicates assessments of microcredit policies and programs. Some observers, for instance, consider programs to be successful if they can produce positive "change" in an entrepreneur's personal income and assets. Others, however, assess success by conducting institutional level analyses, focusing on a program's ability to serve low-income clients in a financially sustainable manner. This chapter reviews arguments related to these two levels of analysis and develops a framework for evaluating the performance of microcredit programs.

INDIVIDUAL-LEVEL ASSESSMENTS

Program assessment at the borrower's level appeals to those who argue that the performance of microcredit programs needs to be gauged by their economic impact on variables such as a borrower's income and assets and by their social impact on variables such as community participation and empowerment.

The need to focus on the social benefits of microcredit programs is considered to be important by many leading microcredit practitioners. For instance, according to Ela Bhatt of India's Self Employed Women's Association (SEWA) program, "poverty is not simply a lack of funds, but . . . vulnerability, powerlessness, and dependency. Development finance institutions that offer only traditional microfinance services are not as effective as institutions that also help borrowers overcome the psychological burdens of poverty" (E. Bhatt, 1998). Indeed, some of the more prominent microfinance programs seem to go beyond the sole provision of financial services.

For instance, the Grameen Bank provides members with information and indirect access to such social inputs as consciousness raising, health and nutrition services, and training in such areas as children's education and sanitation (Khandker, 1996). The SEWA program provides leadership training to women on issues related to political participation, teaching them ways and means of holding community leaders and government officials accountable. Social objectives such as empowerment of women through participation in self-help groups are key to FINCA's village banking methodology (Holt, 1994). The Women's World Banking organization advocates that assisting the poor in community organizing and providing them with appropriate technical training and business assistance is as important as providing them with financial services (Jani and Pedroni, 1997).

The importance of providing poor entrepreneurs with business development services has also been stressed by Dichter (1996) who argues that "without other inputs than credit, a great many micro-loan recipients have enormous difficulty making productive use of these small loans" (p. 262). Arguing that the credit-led strategies have come into vogue largely because NGOs have found themselves under exceeding pressure to become self-sustainable, he points out that programs that act in their own self-interest and stop providing nonfinancial services in order to achieve financial sustainability might not be building sustainable development capacity for the poor.

Given that financial and nonfinancial services may lead to a variety of benefits, many observers advocate that microcredit program appraisals need to capture "change" in well-being at the borrower's level. This has led to a plethora of evaluation efforts that apply a variety of research designs to measure specific economic and social impacts. For example, Benus et al. (1995) use treatment/control groups to evaluate the social benefits and costs of providing microenterprise development assistance—including long-term work-search waivers and access to training, technical assistance, and capital—to Unemployment Insurance recipients in the states of Massachusetts and Washington. The study measures benefits as changes in total earnings due to self- and wage-employment over a 31- to 33-month period. Raheim and Alter (1995) measure net profits accruing to welfare recipients who participated in the national Self-Employment Investment Demonstration. Clark and Kays (1999) and Himes with Servon (1998) conduct longitudinal studies of microcredit recipients to evaluate changes in personal income, household assets, and jobs created.

Researchers have similarly evaluated the impact of microcredit programs in developing countries. For example, Schuler and Hashemi (1994) have employed a quasi-experimental method and a two-stage clustered sampling technique to test the hypotheses that Bangladeshi women borrowers benefit from empowerment and that such empowerment results in higher contraceptive use as compared to nonborrowing women. Hulme et al. (1994) use a cross-sectional survey design to study the impact of credit on the household income and enterprise productivity of borrowers in Sri Lanka's SANASA program. Buvinic et al. (1989) investigate the impact of microcredit on microproducers and microvendors in Ecuador by conducting a longitudinal survey of a group of borrowers, as well as nonborrowers who serve as a control group. The literature reveals that such approaches have also been employed to study the impact of nonfinancial services such as training, technical assistance, and a host of health and human development interventions that are usually provided with credit.

But since most such studies have suffered from one or more methodological problems such as selection bias,[1] lack of control groups,[2] and inability to gather longitudinal data, they have failed to provide evidence that provisions of credit, training, or technical assistance are good uses of scarce public resources (Schreiner, 1999a; Morduch, 1999). For instance, after reviewing Benus et al.'s (1995) evaluation of the Unemployment Insurance Self-Employment Demonstration program in the United States, Schreiner (1999a) concludes that "blanket endorsements of microenterprise programs may be premature. . . . UISED did not reveal how microenterprise programs produce impact nor whether their net social benefits are positive."

Many observers point to the need to measure changes in such dependent variables as income, assets, productivity, self-esteem, and general quality of life that may result from the provision of financial and nonfinancial services. Indeed, they all seem to echo Hulme and Mosley's (1996) declaration that "the ultimate test of any institution is . . . whether . . . it manages to do something useful" (p. 86).

INSTITUTIONAL-LEVEL ASSESSMENTS

The individual-level assessment approach has been questioned by those who believe that the performance of microcredit programs needs to be gauged not by assessing their specific impacts on borrowers but by their impact on the financial system at large. According to Rhyne (1994, p. 107), for example, "If program evaluations can be freed from the burden of proving that finance matters . . . they can concentrate on evaluating the quality of the services and their institutional settings."

This alternative approach to program appraisal is captured in Jacob Yaron's framework for assessing the performance of microcredit institutions. Yaron (1994) recommends employing two key indicators—outreach and sustainability—to analyze program performance. In the spirit of his approach, institutional outreach is measured in terms of its breadth as well as depth. While the breadth of outreach is assessed by measuring such variables as the number of people who are provided financial services and the kinds of products and services offered to them, the depth of outreach is generally measured by the average loan size and the gender distribution of the portfolio. In this regard, the smaller the average loan size and the greater the number of female clients, the higher is the confidence that services are indeed being provided to a low-income clientele.[3]

Rhyne (1994, p. 111) has recommended the assessment of another variable—the quality of service provided. According to her, "The strongest and simplest test of service quality . . . is willingness of clients to pay, which serves as a basic indicator of the value or the benefit of the service." A critical element of such a market test is the measurement of such "program quality" variables as client transaction costs, requests for repeat loans, and ultimately, a program's loan repayment performance.

A second, widely employed measure for assessing the success of a microcredit program is its level of sustainability. According to Yaron (1992, p. 5), self-sustainability is achieved when the return on equity, net of any subsidy received, equals or exceeds the opportunity costs of funds. The extent to which an institution has achieved self-sufficiency is measured by calculating a Subsidy Dependence Index (SDI), which is "a ratio that measures the percentage increase in the average on-lending interest rate required to compensate . . . for the elimination of subsidies in a given year while keeping its return on equity equal to the approximate nonconcessional borrowing cost" (ibid). For example, a positive SDI suggests that a program would need to increase the interest rate it charges on loans in order to break even if it were to pay market prices for the business inputs, including loanable funds, that it uses. In other words, an SDI of 50 percent for a lender charging 20 percent on loans indicates that in order to be sustainable, the interest rate would need to be increased to 30 percent.[4]

Yaron's approach to assessing the success of microfinance programs has been widely adopted. For example, it is employed by Gonzalez-Vega et al. (1997) in their study of the BancoSol program in Bolivia, by Khandkar et al. (1995) in their study of Grameen Bank, and by Christen et al. (1994) in their study of 11 microfinance programs in Indonesia, Bangladesh, Kenya, Senegal, Niger, Costa Rica, Colombia, the Dominican Republic, and Bolivia.

Despite these strongly articulated views, debates continue without consensus between those who advocate the measurement of change by employing methodologies to compare "before" and "after"—and if at all possible, "with" and "without," economic, human, and social capital variables—and others who advocate institutional level assessments for gauging the performance of microcredit programs.

Those who support and oppose each of the above views often argue about whether microcredit programs justify public support because they deliver social benefits, or whether movements away from subsidies and toward financial and operational self-sufficiency need to be emphasized by sponsors and aid agencies

(Nelson, 1994). These discussions often tend to reduce the meaning of program viability to the issue of subsidy dependence versus subsidy independence, with the latter generally preferred over the former. In other words, a high degree of subsidy independence is suggested by some as a proxy for program viability and as a sign of a program being operationally disciplined and efficient.

But a singular focus on subsidy independence as an evaluative measure of program efficiency can be inappropriate (Morduch, 2000). This is because it fails to differentiate between external and internal efficiency, and assumes that the former means or implies the latter. This is not so (Bhatt and Tang, forthcoming).

External efficiency refers to the benefits/costs ratio achieved by a microcredit project as compared with those of other similar development interventions. It would be relatively easy to evaluate the external efficiency of a profit-oriented program if the formal financial market could be used as a benchmark for evaluation. Nevertheless, although some microfinance institutions like ACCION International have tried to link their operations to the world financial market by reselling their loan portfolios in secondary markets, the vast majority of existing programs, especially those operating in the United States, are far from achieving even operational self-sufficiency. As a matter of fact, all programs in the United States are still reliant on public/private subsidies in one form or another. For these programs, the key is to determine whether, when these schemes are put side by side with other programs, the welfare gains associated with these schemes justify the public outlay.

Internal efficiency, on the other hand, refers to the ability of a program to deliver specific services at minimum costs. Experiences from around the world suggest that programs are rendered nonviable due to internal inefficiencies which can result from a number of factors: the inability or unwillingness to cater to the target market; lending to individuals who do not have adequate debt capacity; lack of understanding of the factors that are critical to minimizing delinquencies and defaults; and inability of sponsors and aid agencies to provide appropriate technical assistance to funded programs.

Internal efficiency is critical to the viability of all kinds of programs: those that are self-sufficient, as well as those that are not. Programs that are internally inefficient and aspire to become self-sufficient will find it difficult to break even financially, since they will incur as well as impose high transaction costs in approving and disbursing loans. On the other hand, programs that are internally efficient do not necessarily have to be profit oriented or motivated; they may be serving a clientele and providing services that indeed do require subsidies, but this has no theoretical bearing on their cost minimization efforts (Morduch, 2000).

Some observers might argue that it is conceivable that even internally inefficient programs can serve socially useful purposes that could justify subsidies, and even their short-term existence. For example, a hypothetical program could lose 50 percent of its portfolio; yet if one of its hundred clients created a hundred jobs, the social benefits attained might justify the costs of defaults as well as loan-fund capitalization and administration. Although such social cost-benefit analysis might indeed justify the support received by such a program, accounts of microcredit programs worldwide rarely provide examples of inefficient programs producing such success stories. On the contrary, there is strong evidence that clients of internally efficient programs (which does not necessarily imply unsubsidized) exhibit financial discipline, especially in terms of making timely repayments and pressuring peer borrowers to do the same. Over time, the managers of such stable institutions win the confidence of their borrowers. Borrowers then become savers, trusting the program with their deposits. This increases the public's sense of association with and ownership in the program, factors that are key to building long-term client relationships.

Based on these perspectives, we argue that internal efficiency is fundamental to program viability, and we emphasize the need for sustainability not because subsidy independence is a necessary condition, but "because of the need for stable (microcredit) institutions with viable prospects beyond the short term" (Von Pischke et al., 1997, p. 18).

CONSTRAINTS, CONTEXTS, AND CONDITIONS

In this book, the performance of microcredit programs is assessed by investigating the entrepreneurial *constraints* faced by microentrepreneurs, the *contexts* necessary for achieving superior loan repayment performance, and the *conditions* that are necessary for program sustainability.

In order to establish the vital and complex linkages among *constraints*, *contexts*, and *conditions*,[5] we adopt a cross-disciplinary perspective to problem analysis, building our case by drawing from research in the areas of entrepreneurship, economic development, sociology, anthropology, and political science. Such an approach, often labeled the New Institutional Economics (NIE), emphasizes the role of formal and informal constraints, including those structured by cultural norms, traditions, and conventions, in predicting human behavior and institutional performance (Furubotn and Richter, 1997; Lin and Nugent, 1995; North, 1990; Ostrom et al., 1993).

Specifically, the NIE literature focuses on the relationship between configurations of rules and incentive structures on the one hand and their impact on collective action and transaction cost problems on the other (Eggertsson, 1990; Ostrom, 1997;

Williamson, 1985). It argues that different communities around the world face unique economic, legal, and cultural environments which produce different expectations regarding the kind of behavior that is permitted and prohibited (Ostrom, 1990). Since institutional performance depends on the specificity of such environments at the "macro" level, as well as the configuration of transactional arrangements at the "micro" level, different combinations of macro- and microlevel factors result in different incentive structures and, as a result, different outcomes. It is unlikely that design features that make for a successful program in one setting will automatically produce similar outcomes in another.

We analyze the viability of microcredit programs by drawing the following arguments from the above literature: (1) the constraints faced by the target market determine the kinds of financial and nonfinancial inputs needed for entrepreneurship development; (2) the socioeconomic and institutional contexts within which programs operate are important determinants of their loan repayment performance; and (3) the conditions under which programs carry out financial, social, and administrative intermediation determine their long-term sustainability.

Constraints: Most Third World microcredit programs operate on the *a priori* assumption that it is the lack of capital that constrains entrepreneurship development. Indeed, due to the large scale and immense absorptive capacity of the informal sector, even small capital inputs from microlenders may result in large positive impacts for small-scale entrepreneurs in developing countries. Due to the ready availability of markets for their products and services, microentrepreneurs are often able to put small amounts of capital to productive use immediately. Further, returns on investment are high enough to allow for the repayment of loans and enhancement of personal income.

But such a scenario is seldom true for informal sector entrepreneurs in the United States. First and foremost, the United States has what is largely a formal sector economy; the total number of formal and informal microenterprises account for 6 to 20 percent of the market, as compared to the 60 to 80 percent of the market in developing countries (Edgcomb et al., 1996). Wage jobs are comparatively abundant in the United States, and the few informal sector entrepreneurs that do exist find survival extremely difficult, not so much because they are capital constrained (Balkin, 1989a, p. 169; Schreiner, 1998),[6] but because their productivity is low and they do not have access to the kinds of densely populated markets that are available in rural Bangladesh or urban Peru. Table 2.1 provides examples of the goods and services produced by microentrepreneurs in the United States and abroad. Microentrepreneurs in the United States face fierce competition from "big name" providers for many of the activities listed in the left-hand column. On the other hand, Third World consumers in rural villages and urban barrios depend almost entirely on informal sector entrepreneurs in order to consume the products and services listed in the right-hand column.

The lack of markets, for example, in the case of street vendors in New York or Los Angeles, is partly due to how the goods and services are produced, which might be considered unhealthful by many potential customers. It is also due to the fact that since informal sector activities such as street vending are illegal in most parts of the country, there exists an inherent prejudice in the mind of the public regarding such informal entrepreneurs. For these reasons, unlike consumers in developing countries, Americans do not spend much of their budget on products and services offered by microentrepreneurs (Schreiner, 1998). As such, credits made available to such informal sector entrepreneurs in the United States do not result in the leveraged economic returns obtained by some microlenders in the Third World.

Recognizing the legal difficulties associated with informal entrepreneurship as well as the challenges associated with selling informal sector goods and services, a number of microcredit programs in the United States target not informal sector entrepreneurs but the "lifestyle entrepreneurs," that is, individuals who either want to start a formal sector-based microbusiness or grow an existing enterprise, on a full-time or part-time basis.

Table 2.1. Microenterprise activities in the United States and abroad

United States	Abroad
Care for children or pets	Plant crops and fatten livestock
Cut hair or polish nails	Do odd jobs, especially on farms
Cook and sell food and drinks	Cook and sell food and drinks
Sell Avon, Amway, or Mary Kay	Petty trade in food, clothes, or toiletries
Clean homes, cars, or offices	Take in laundry
Trade and/or repair clothes or cars	Make and/or repair clothes or cars
Paint or repair houses	Build or repair houses
Cut grass or trim branches	Collect and sell wood, charcoal, or water
Kill pests	Carry loads or messages
Repossess cars	Drive a bus or truck
Work with wood	Work with wood or metal
Rent videotapes	Show movies from videotapes
Deejay parties	Play in a band
Drive cabs	Run a rickshaw
Quilt or knit blankets	Husk rice or shell peanuts
Sling newspapers or brochures	Sell newspapers or lottery tickets
Make and sell arts and crafts	Scavenge for things to recycle
Buy and sell drugs	Shine or repair shoes

Source: Schreiner (1998)

But even for these individuals, capital inputs may not be the binding constraint to enterprise development and growth. For example, in their study of 16 microenterprise development programs, Else and Clay-Thompson (1998) found that the initial assumption of program designers—that capital was *the* constraint to entrepreneurship development—was inaccurate. According to them "over 40 percent of the business starts began without accessing funds from the microenterprise organizations or their commercial credit linkages. . . . In fact, the greatest need for many was not capital, but training and technical assistance" (p. 5). These entrepreneurs may also face difficulties in accessing and gathering information about business licenses, permits, and taxes, all of which ultimately increase the cost of doing business.

A similar observation has been made by Balkin (1989b). According to him, the financing "aspect of encouraging low-income people to start small businesses has received too much emphasis. The biggest problem is not how people can receive loans to start their businesses. The biggest problem is to set in place policies and a system whereby . . . people obtain the information with ease to begin self-employment activity" (pp. 121–122).

These and other similar studies suggest that an exclusive focus on capital and neglect of other important factor-inputs is inappropriate when entrepreneurs face low levels of revenues and profits due to high input costs, weak market demand, and competition from "brand name" providers of products and services.

Contexts: A community's socioeconomic and institutional contexts are critical for minimizing loan default rates—perhaps the single most important factor that can render loan programs nonviable.

Microcredit programs that are successful in developing countries make use of the unique socioeconomic contexts that exist, say, in areas such as urban barrios and rural villages. The socio-economic profile of many village-communities in India is characterized by poor women entrepreneurs engaged in activities such as basket weaving or hog fattening. Small amounts of capital can enhance their ability to make productive investments in the short run and reduce their otherwise high vulnerability to consumption-shocks (Khandker, 1996; Morduch, 1998). Because of the benefits of microcredit, women borrowers in developing countries are increasingly dependent on future loans for both enterprise and household development. This high value placed on future loans plays an important role in combating the moral hazard problem and ensuring that the lender gets repaid.

When one contrasts the United States context with that of the Third World, several critical differences emerge. First, for most low-income people in the United States, the degree of usefulness of the loan is not as high as it is for informal sector entrepreneurs in, say, Bangladesh. The ready availability of social safety nets such as government welfare programs, as well as the abundance of charitable and humanitarian relief agencies that can provide basic necessities such as food, clothing, and shelter should people face economic adversities, makes business failure and nonrepayment of borrowed money less costly than for microentrepreneurs in the Third World.[7] Indeed, the safety net in the United States may reduce the incentives to succeed in self-employment in several ways (Schreiner, 1998):

> First, the safety net prevents starvation. This reduces the push toward self-employment. Second, welfare requires less risk and less effort than self-employment. Regardless of how much the owner of a new ME [microenterprise] works, it may still fail. Third, income limits set by welfare programs reduce the rewards to the risk and effort of self-employment. Someone on welfare who starts to draw income from an ME

will get less public assistance unless the ME has its own legal status that puts a firewall between business and personal income. A fourth and related point is that asset limits set by welfare programs discourage saving. . . . The problem is less that limits on income and assets disqualify people for public assistance and more that the limits kick in before the ME can support the owner. (pp. 12–13)

Second, many microcredit program participants in the United States do not belong to the "entrepreneurial poor" category, which, in the Third World context, generally implies at least a couple of years of experience in running a small-scale venture that generates positive cash flow. Such program participants are start-up entrepreneurs who have ideas, not existing businesses. The lack of relevant business experience, for instance, of welfare recipients, coupled with their usually limited education and skills, severely restricts their entrepreneurial capacity and ability to make the right business decisions in the extremely competitive markets within which they operate.

In addition to differences in the socioeconomic characteristics of borrowers, the institutional context within which most U.S. programs operate is different too. Key factors that account for the success of the best Third World microcredit programs—the ability of lenders to reduce borrower transaction costs, the high reserves of community social capital and reciprocity, and fear of sanctions in the event of default—are seldom achieved or encountered in most U.S. contexts.

First, lenders are unable to provide borrowers the convenience and transaction cost reduction features that characterize overseas lending programs. This is because implementing Grameen Bank–style decentralized branch operations and mobile banking units is resource intensive and increases the already high costs of administering small loans. Further, unlike overseas programs where loan applications are often only one page long, the loan application process in most U.S. programs is lengthy, cumbersome, and bureaucratic, especially when the funds being disbursed come from special government programs that require extensive "client eligibility" documentation.

Second, unsecured and joint-liability lending to entrepreneurs who are selected on the basis of socioeconomic "homogeneity" is highly risky given the low levels of social cohesion and reciprocity in many inner-city neighborhoods. When members of groups that have low social capital default, whether it is because of opportunism or project failure, their peers seldom want to make good on the loan repayment. Although it is widely assumed that borrower-group homogeneity helps to reduce lender risk and accounts for the superior loan repayment performance of credit groups (Devereux and Fishe, 1993; Desai, 1982; Huppi and Feder, 1990), such claims are questionable. Analytical advances in the New Institutional Economics literature (Furubotn and Richter, 1997; Lin and Nugent, 1995; Tang, 1992), especially in the rational choice theory of collective action (Ostrom, 1998), suggest that homogeneity of credit groups might not account for low default rates. In fact, field studies conducted by Hulme and Mosley (1996) and Zeller (1998) provide evidence that group homogeneity does not correlate positively with loan repayment performance.

Third, borrowers in many U.S. microcredit programs have little fear of being "sanctioned" should they default on the loans. Although the incentives associated with getting larger loans in the future make many microcredit programs successful overseas, research suggests that disincentives to default probably play an equally important role in ensuring borrower compliance with group and program rules (Hulme and Mosley, 1996). Such disincentives are often the result of possible sanctioning from the community or from the program.

As regards the former case, in the Third World context, such sanctioning mechanisms include community ostracism, public embarrassment, and loss of social standing—reputational assets that are key to conducting economic transactions (Besley, 1995). But communities in the United States, especially those within the inner cities, seldom rely on social cohesiveness or reputational assets for conducting day-to-day business. The fear of community sanctions is often insufficient to deter default among borrowers under such circumstances.

As regards the latter case, a program's sanctioning mechanisms can include probation instruments—generally implying some sort of legal action against the defaulter,[8] as well as the threat of loss of access to future services, such as technical assistance, credit, or savings facilities (Stiglitz and Weiss, 1983). Where such disincentives are effective overseas, potential defaulters perceive the costs of default as exceeding the benefits. Further, they perceive the sanctioning threats as credible, because the threats are actually enforced by the lenders. This in turn sends a signal to both current and prospective borrowers that the threats are not just "cheap talk" but are indeed carried out.

But as is demonstrated in the following chapters, many nonviable microcredit programs in the United States have failed to create a disciplined lending environment, as a result of which there has existed little fear of sanctions among borrowers. Program participants have perceived lending officers and managers as lax and often incompetent, especially in tracking loan repayments, enforcing rules, and taking defaulters to task. This has sent a negative signal to the community and has resulted in a culture of late payments and loan defaults. Overall, the ability and/or willingness to operate in an efficient, businesslike fashion—a factor that is key to the effectiveness of successful overseas initiatives such as ACCION International—has been markedly absent in the operations of many U.S. microcredit programs.

Conditions: What conditions are necessary for program sustainability? Three key areas—social intermediation, financial intermediation, and administrative intermediation—merit attention.

Social intermediation: This is the process of interacting with and organizing prospective borrowers to build their human capital so that they may become "loan ready" (Bennett and Goldberg, 1993). Doing so has been challenging in the United States because of client outreach and recruitment problems on the one hand, and the limited impact of human capital building interventions such as training classes on the other hand. The consequent inability of microcredit programs to serve sufficient numbers of clients with "cash flowing" businesses and adequate debt capacity often renders them unsustainable.

Financial intermediation: This generally refers to lending and deposit-taking activities of financial institutions. Problems in financial intermediation arise from the inability of lenders to manage risks and reduce costs of transactions. For example, the U.S. development community has not been able to assess the true risks associated with joint-liability lending in many inner-city communities, and as a result, most joint-liability programs have not enhanced programs' loan repayment and administrative efficiency. A key reason is the unwillingness of borrowers to internalize the otherwise high risks and costs associated with making small loans (Bhatt and Tang, 1998a). When microcredit programs make unsecured loans to entrepreneurs in communities with low social capital, and when information on credit and character history is difficult to obtain—as is often the case with immigrant populations—formal rules, policies, and procedures are devised and imposed to constrain borrower opportunism at every stage of credit delivery. It is the very high administrative costs incurred by microcredit programs in such situations that present a significant challenge to sustainability.

Administrative intermediation: This refers to the practices, policies, and governance structures that a lending agency assumes in order to run its operations. Most problems in administrative intermediation arise when the incentive structures facing the various stakeholders—including borrowers, field staff, program managers, boards of directors, and sponsors—are not aligned. Programs receiving funds from various sources, for example, often need to cater to different donor expectations. Balancing multiple missions, program deliverables, and reporting requirements, especially when funders are both public and private entities, often leads to operational inefficiencies.

In the chapters that follow, the framework and arguments developed above are employed to analyze the performance of microcredit programs in the United States. Although not stated explicitly, in addition to assessing existing programs, most elements of the framework are also useful for designing future microcredit initiatives. Whether it be the assessment of current programs or the design of new ones, three elements are integral to the process. The first involves understanding the nature of the constraints and opportunities faced by people in developing their enterprises. This allows for an identification of the financial and nonfinancial barriers to entrepreneurship. The second involves understanding the socioeconomic and institutional contexts within which a program is or will be located. This allows policy makers to design programs that can achieve superior loan repayment performance. These two elements impact the third—the conditions under which the program is or will be operating. This allows for the identification of possible challenges in social, financial, and administrative intermediation.

NOTES

1. The goal of sampling is to select a subset of a population with a distribution of characteristics that matches the population. Such a subset is said to be a representative sample. Selection bias is a flaw in the sampling process that results in an over- or under-representation of some segments of the population in the sample.

2. The following discussion of control groups in microcredit programs is based on Schreiner (1999a&c). Evaluators use control groups to assess cause and effect. They seek to isolate the impact of a specific service, such as the provision of credit or training. The intent is to analyze what would have happened to users in the absence of the service by measuring, for example, income and asset levels over time for two groups—one that actually receives the credit or training (the experimental, or "with," group), and one that does not (the control, or "without," group).

In principle, the classic control group comprises people who apply for a program, are found to be eligible for its services given a program's screening test (for example, Grameen Bank's policy is to lend only to those applicants who own less than half a hectare of land), but are excluded for purposes of the experiment. In practice, due to the time and resource intensive nature of such experiments, as well as concerns about their being unethical (some needy people may be excluded due to the random assignment), such control group experiments are seldom conducted (one notable exception is the Unemployment Insurance Self-Employment Demonstration, see Benus et al., 1995). Instead, some analysts prefer to use "comparison" group experiments, in which the users' observable socioeconomic traits (such as gender, age, education, occupation, assets) are matched with a group of individuals who have not requested services, and changes in impact variables are compared over time. See, for example, Raheim and Alter (1998).

3. Some observers argue that average loan size may be an imperfect measure of depth of outreach (personal communication, Jonathan Morduch, May, 2000).

4. According to Hulme and Mosley (1996), when raising interest rates is politically impossible or financially risky (if the level of competition is

such as to deprive a program of its market if rates go too high), the necessary adjustment to achieve sustainability has to come from the cost side.

5. Most evaluative studies of enterprise development programs tend to focus on the constraints faced by the target population, the repayment performance of the microcredit programs, and the sustainability of such initiatives separately. Since these studies are often carried out for different programs, and often across vastly dissimilar contextual settings, the linkages between the needs and profiles of the populations served, the loan repayment performance of the programs, and their ability to sustain themselves are often left unclear.

Morrisson et al. (1994), for example, survey 300 small-scale entrepreneurs from seven countries in Africa, Latin America, and Asia to assess constraints faced by them due to excessive government regulations, taxes, labor laws, and lack of access to capital. Although one of their key recommendations is that the government play a more active role in addressing the financial constraints of the entrepreneurs, their study does not evaluate any existing programs that serve such entrepreneurs.

While some program evaluations do analyze the performance of specific programs, and link them to the needs of the markets being served, they seldom address how performance factors such as loan repayment rates and their determinants impact program sustainability. For example, although Sharma and Zeller's (1997) study of three Bangladeshi programs underscores that services should be "tailored" such that it becomes worthwhile for the poor to establish a profitable long-term relationship with the lending institution (p. 1740), it does not address the issues of how programs might adjust their services to improve loan repayment performance and what the provision of nonfinancial services might mean to program sustainability.

Finally, while a number of studies assess the sustainability and cost-effectiveness of microcredit programs, they shed little light on design features that can enhance loan repayment performance. For instance, Edgcomb et al.'s (1996) rigorous study of six microcredit programs in the United States does not analyze factors related to the loan repayment performance of the initiatives investigated. Although the research effort provides valuable information on such performance indicators as cost per loan disbursed, cost per client assisted, and cost per job created, it provides little information that can be used for the design of future programs.

6. According to Balkin (1989a), the financing aspects of cultivating self-employment have received "too much emphasis." He argues, "Many businesses do not require a great deal of start-up capital, and many low-income persons could generate that small amount of capital on their own" (p. 169).

7. Safety nets such as welfare programs may hinder entrepreneurship development. For example, asset limits set by welfare programs have discouraged savings, which are critical to new venture creation and growth.

8. This might not be in a formal court of law but before elected, informal village bodies, such as the *Gram Panchayats* of India, that serve as local judicial units.

CHAPTER THREE

Rationale

M any scholars argue that microcredit programs are designed on the questionable assumptions that it is the lack of capital that constrains enterprise development, and, further, that small-scale entrepreneurs experience a capital crunch owing to the discriminatory lending practices of conventional banks. Two reasons are forwarded to support this view (Bates, 1997; Davis, 1995; Laguerre, 1998; Price and Monroe, 1991). First, ventures generally fail not due to the lack of capital but because entrepreneurs lack business planning, management, and marketing skills. Second, a struggle for resources such as capital is key to ensuring the survival of the most creative and viable ideas.[1] Since most conventional lenders are unwilling to "bet" on a business idea that is untested, most entrepreneurs use informally acquired financing and personal savings during the start-up phases of enterprise development.

The first argument suggests that entrepreneurs who lack human capital in the form of business and problem-solving skills are usually at a competitive disadvantage in the marketplace and will not succeed even if they are provided with credit by financial institutions. This view has led to calls for expanding training and technical assistance programs to build the entrepreneurial and business management capacities of entrepreneurs.

The second argument is made by those who believe that the lack of social capital in the form of personal and business networks prevents many entrepreneurs from identifying financing sources (Giles, 1993). Communities that possess high reserves of social capital may find it easier to access capital, for example, from informal sources such as family and friends. This perspective has led to calls for making community building an integral part of economic development strategies (Fettig, 1996; Putnam, 1993b). In addition, the above argument underscores the need to encourage savings in low-income communities. This has led to the development of innovative initiatives such as Individual Development Accounts (IDAs) that foster asset accumulation among low-income entrepreneurs by providing them with access and incentives to save.[2]

We conducted an exploratory study of 103 microentrepreneurs who were turned down for loans during the past 12 months to examine (1) the extent to which the lack of capital was perceived as a constraint on enterprise development, and (2) what the determinants of such capital constraints might be. Given that there seems to be an emerging consensus among policy makers that it is the limited access to capital, especially due to the stringency of bank underwriting, that constrains microenterprise development, this analysis has significant implications.

For instance, if entrepreneurs identify the lack of capital as a barrier to enterprise development and have the capacity to generate enough cash flow to service debt, then the arguments presented by supporters of credit-led development programs might get support. On the other hand, if noncapital factors such as lack of business information, skills, and revenues, are also identified as being important, it might warrant an examination of how and to what extent enterprise development programs can assist small-scale entrepreneurs in these areas. Further, if entrepreneurs are unable to access bank financing despite having viable business proposals, then arguments favoring programs that assess risk in more appropriate ways, and make loans available by relaxing credit and collateral requirements, might get support. But if financing requests are turned down due to the high risks of the ventures, strategies for increasing the market viability and efficiency of microenterprises merit attention.

The plan for the rest of the chapter is as follows. First we discuss the theoretical importance of capital in enterprise development. This is followed by an investigation of factors that constrain small-scale entrepreneurs and the determinants of capital constraints faced by these entrepreneurs. Finally, after a brief discussion of our hypotheses and data, we present the findings from our survey, along with their implications for microcredit program design.

IMPORTANCE OF CAPITAL
IN ENTERPRISE DEVELOPMENT

Many scholars have studied the role of capital in entrepreneurship and economic development (Eswaran and Kotwal, 1986; Feder, 1990; Fry, 1995). The general implications of such studies are that lack of capital can impact small-scale entrepreneurs at both the firm and household levels.

It has been suggested, for example, that capital constraints have negative effects on firm productivity, product choice, and labor supply (Eswaran and Kotwal, 1986; Feder, 1990; Tella, 1969). Financially constrained enterprises behave like risk-averse individuals (Greenwald and Stiglitz, 1990). Ventures that are capital restricted refrain from investing in creative and innovative processes that are characteristic of small and microenterprises. By extension, households whose incomes are primarily derived from entrepreneurship may perceive such "innovative" activities as being unsuited to a smooth flow of consumption. As a result, these households focus more on low-risk, low-return types of ventures. Given a set of individuals with similar risk preferences, those who can access greater amounts of consumption credit will have a greater capacity to absorb risk (Eswaran and Kotwal, 1986). These arguments assume greater importance in the context of low-income entre-preneurs who are self-employed and who often do not distinguish between the activities and finances of their ventures and their households.

BARRIERS TO ENTREPRENEURSHIP

Research suggests that four factors—lack of capital, information, management skills, and sales—typically constrain small-scale entrepreneurs.

Lack of capital: Many scholars have examined the capital con-straints faced by entrepreneurs within the inner city, especially in terms of barriers to obtaining working capital for purchas-ing inventory or financing labor, and fixed capital for purchasing equipment. Most studies point to the discriminatory behavior of traditional banks as being the key determinant of lack of access to capital. Perhaps the most revealing of such efforts is that of Dymski and Veitch (1996), who systematically argue that over the years, banks have established their own niches that focus on serving the "better off" customers, and on excluding those who live in low-income neighborhoods.

They point out, for instance, that in 1993, there were more bank branches in the highest 40 percent income census tracts of Los Angeles than there were in the lowest 60 percent, even though the population of the latter region was 1.5 times that of the former region (see table 3.1). Their assessment of bank closures and openings between 1988 and 1993 in low-income and high-income areas seems to confirm that low-income communities were being systematically "redlined" by the formal banking sector.

Branches closed in high-income areas had more nearby branches than did branches closed in low-income areas, suggesting that these closures were simply responses to increased competition during the period. There was, however, a substantial presence of check-cashing stores near closed branches in the lowest-income census tracts. This suggests that although a significant demand for financial services remained, banks simply withdrew from low-income areas. (p. 51)

The authors make similar observations with regard to bank branch openings (see table 3.2).

New branches are clustered in the highest income census tracts near where other branches were already open; they are seldom near any second-tier financial firms. A comparison of the nearby-branch statistics for branch closures and openings shows, further, that branch openings occurred on average in areas already more densely covered with branches than did branch closures. Evidently, banks locate where their competitors already are or are moving to.

[There is] . . . a spatial separation between the formal banking sector—in ever hotter pursuit of upscale customers—
and the second-tier financial sector. (p. 53)

This separation has led to second-tier financial institutions
such as check-cashing outlets and pawnbrokers playing an important role in filling the existing credit gap (Caskey, 1994). Stoesz
and Saunders (1999, p. 397) cite investigative journalist Michael
Hudson to reveal that revenues of businesses that "bottom-feed"
on the fringe economy are probably $200 billion to $300 billion
a year. But observers such as Dymski and Veitch (1996, p. 53)
argue that check cashers, for instance, cannot provide a safe
place for deposits or the opportunity to earn interest. Instead, the
high costs of their services and the "households' deaccumulation
of their stock of assets to meet current income crises" prevent
these so-called "fringe banks" from facilitating sustainable enterprise development.

Table 3.1. Distribution of financial services in Los Angeles by census
tract median income

1990 Median Income	Bank Branches	Credit Unions	Check Cashers	Pawn-brokers	1990 Population
Lowest 60% income census tracts	280	51	162	100	2,433,177
Highest 40% income census tracts	294	20	18	15	1,497,749

Source: Dymski and Veitch (1996), p. 51.

Table 3.2. Density of financial services around bank branches closed and opened, 1988–1993

1990 MEDIAN INCOME	BANK BRANCHES	CHECK CASHERS	TOTAL BRANCHES CLOSED
Lowest 20% income census tracts	3	3	22 of 38 (58%)
Highest 20% income census tracts	4	0	55 of 189 (29%)
1990 MEDIAN INCOME	BANK BRANCHES	CHECK CASHERS	TOTAL BRANCHES OPENED
Lowest 20% income census tracts	17	1	9 of 38 (24%)
Highest 20% income census tracts	6	0	28 of 189 (15%)

Source: Dymski and Veitch (1996), p. 52.
Note: Numbers represent the median number of financial firms of each type within a one-mile radius of the bank branch closed during 1988 to 1993.

Lack of information: Access to business information plays a crucial role in microenterprise development. According to Casson (1982), for instance:

- An entrepreneur needs information on profit opportunities from various sources.
- Networks of family and friends are valuable sources of low-cost information.
- Clubs and societies are also key sources that can acquire information and make it available to the entrepreneur at low cost.
- Feedback of information from past activities is crucial to the long-term success of an enterprise.

Casson's theoretical framework has been verified by a number of scholars, especially in the context of the informational advantages possessed by immigrant entrepreneurs. Some observers, for example, have argued that ethnic networks feed economic information to prospective entrepreneurs about which industries are best to enter and what the barriers to entry might be (Wells, 1991). Such access to information about business opportunities and resources is key to identifying market niches and coordinating resources to exploit market opportunities. The ability to do so makes the entrepreneur different, allowing her to gain a competitive advantage in the marketplace.

Lack of management skills: Small-scale ventures can fail not only due to the lack of capital but also because entrepreneurs lack business management skills. Research suggests that the failure rate for those entering self-employment from unemployment is twice as high as for those who were previously employed (Evans and Leighton, 1990). Some studies show that the propensity for self-employment, especially in immigrant communities, increases with higher levels of business management skills (Yuengert, 1992).

The lack of management skills, coupled with the lack of business planning, lead to a number of problems in venture start-up and growth, especially in the areas of market research, product/service delivery, and accounting and financial controls (Scott, 1986, p. 42; Timmons, 1985). This often results in problems such as insufficient cash flow, and the inability to pay suppliers, service debt, and run the day-to-day operations of the business.

Lack of sales: This is perhaps one of the most important factors that lead to the demise of microenterprises.[3] Two factors usually account for the lack of sales. The first is the lack of a market for the goods or services being provided by the entrepreneur. For example, a microentrepreneur who sells mousetraps in a community that is rodent-free will likely experience a paucity of sales. The second challenge is related to creating value in an existing market. This problem is especially pronounced for individuals engaged in small-scale retailing and wholesaling. For example, entrepreneurs such as sidewalk vendors who sell food products and toys, and owners of gift shops and jewelry outlets, find it hard to create value in the marketplace. In fact, some observers might argue that their activities are not entrepreneurial in the traditional economic sense.[4] The large number of providers of these services, especially in the formal sector, often makes it very difficult for the entrepreneurs to generate a critical mass of customers and revenues to make the venture sustainable over the long term.

The constraints faced by entrepreneurs in one or more of the four areas—lack of capital, information, management skills, and sales—are often related to gender, education, and ethnicity (Cooper and Gascon, 1992). For instance, women face greater challenges than men in launching and growing a business. Coping with business and family-related issues and commitments on the one hand, and discrimination in the labor market on the other, often constrains their efforts at entrepreneurship. Unfavorable societal perceptions regarding their entrepreneurial abilities place them at a further disadvantage.

An entrepreneur's ethnicity also impacts the chances of success. Certain Asian ethnic groups, such as the Indian Gujaratis and Parsis have inherent advantages in entrepreneurship due to previous entrepreneurial or business management experiences in their home countries (Light et al., 1993). Some studies suggest that while Korean entrepreneurs find it relatively easier to access capital due to their strong ethnic networks, African Americans are generally unable to borrow start-up capital from family and friends (Fratoe, 1988; Min, 1993).

Finally, higher levels of education enhance the likelihood of success by providing entrepreneurs the knowledge and problem-solving skills needed for starting and operating a business (Bates, 1994; Yoon, 1991). Some studies suggest that Korean and Caribbean contractors in New York City have succeeded because of educational advantages that facilitated their access to clients and jobs; African American contractors are lacking in these areas, and hence have had to struggle to stay in business (Waldinger, 1995).

Although the lack of capital, information, management skills, and sales often combine to constrain enterprise development, most discussions of barriers to venture creation and growth focus almost exclusively on the entrepreneurs' inability to access capital.

BARRIERS TO CAPITAL ACCESS

Entrepreneurs can be constrained in their search for capital due to the lack of conventional financing, the lack of human capital, and the lack of supportive social networks.

Conventional capital constraints: Perhaps the most commonly mentioned constraint facing small-scale entrepreneurs is the lack of access to conventional bank financing (Jordon, 1993). Some observers have suggested that the stringent underwriting criteria employed by banks have led to exclusion of minority entrepreneurs from capital markets (Dymski, 1993). As mentioned earlier in this chapter, such bank "stringency" is often characterized as "redlining," which refers to the practice of turning down loan applications that originate from entrepreneurs residing or operating businesses in low-income areas, such as those of the inner city. In his account of bank redlining, Dreier

(1991), describes the financial crisis that confronted inner-city residents in the late 1980s thus:

> Widening economic disparity between suburbs and cities evolved, along with deepening fiscal crises in the nation's older cities. . . . [N]eighborhood residents and small business owners began to discern a red pen in the invisible hand of the market—especially in the pattern of bank lending decisions. Banks were refusing to make . . . business loans to certain neighborhoods, creating a self-fulfilling prophecy of neglect and deterioration. Moreover, these decisions were based on subjective perceptions—bankers' views of certain neighborhoods as risky—rather than on objective reality. Small businesses were unable to obtain loans to start or expand their operation; . . . neighborhoods were experiencing systematic disinvestment, not isolated lending decisions by individual loan officers. (p. 16)

What are the causes of redlining? From a banker's perspective, redlining is a rational response given the inability to make prudent lending decisions because of the "high-risk" characteristics of the borrower. Specifically, it is related to the low probability of loan repayment on deals that originate from individuals with three key characteristics—tainted credit histories, lack of tangible collateral, and inadequate business profitabilities.[5]

Since lending involves a promise on the part of the borrower to pay in the future, it involves risk. This is because, in general, "when a borrower approaches a lender for a loan, the lender is at an informational disadvantage. The borrower may have spent years working on a project which now requires financing. The lender knows little or nothing about either the project or the borrower" (Fry, 1995, pp. 304–305). In trying to minimize the risk of loan default, lenders rely on certain borrower charac-teristics that serve as "signals" of future repayment behavior.

A key signal of a potential "problem deal" for bankers is an applicant with a tainted credit history. This is because credit his-tories reflect an individual's historical discipline in meeting financial obligations. A good credit history helps the lender to overcome informational disadvantages before the loan contract is approved. But even if the applicant's credit history is perfect, there is no guarantee that the borrower will abide by the contract and repay the loan, because a borrower does not have the same incentive to look after other people's money as he has to look after his own. Bankers get around this "moral hazard" problem by asking for tangible collateral and equity contributions to the loan applicant's business. The intent is to make the debt contract incentive compatible, by aligning the incentives of the borrower more closely with the incentives of the lender. In successful Third World programs, for example, such incentives include offering borrowers larger and repeat loans.

Another signal of a potentially risky loan is a venture with an unproven track record. A track record is usually assessed by an entrepreneur's experience in the specific line of business, as well as a firm's historical revenues and profitability. Ventures that have been unprofitable or that demonstrate weak profit potential (bankers usually assess profit potential by researching market conditions and the entrepreneur's management capacity) are usually poor credit risks. This is a key reason why most successful Third World microcredit programs prefer to lend to the entrepreneurial poor—individuals who have experience in self-employment activities. It also explains why lenders make it a priority to "retain" clients who exhibit financial discipline by paying back several short-term loans. Lending officers actually "construct" a financial history for each borrower from scratch, and over time, these statistics are used for making lending decisions should individuals apply for larger loans in the future.

Human capital constraints: Entrepreneurs who lack human capital are likely to face barriers in trying to raise capital (Bates, 1997; Sanders and Nee, 1996). This argument finds its roots in the disadvantage theory of entrepreneurship, according to which low-income individuals, including many recent immigrants, "congregate in the self-employment market because they are otherwise handicapped. Poor language, limited education and inadequate skills are typical barriers that can exclude newcomers" from capital sources (Tsukashima, 1991, p. 337).

Formal and informal education may help individuals overcome such barriers. For example, entrepreneurship research in the United States suggests that higher levels of education increase the chances of new enterprise survival and growth (Vesper, 1980, pp. 27–55). While many observers underscore the importance of hands-on education acquired by participation in the labor market, some stress the importance of participation in business training programs for learning the basics of entrepreneurship and small-business management (Bender et al., 1990; Borjas, 1986; Timmons, 1985, pp. 179–201). Others underscore the importance of formal schooling and college education (Bates, 1994). According to Sage (1993), for instance:

> Education is a generally agreed upon correlate for success in business. More of it, and not necessarily in business specialties, tends to encourage success. Given the nature of entrepreneurship as a problem solving activity, you would expect that more education would aid in the discipline of problem solving. Much of the success in business entails the ability to identify a particular market niche and then

employ problem solving skills to marshall the resources to adequately address the market. (p. 67)

That human capital is a key determinant of entrepreneurial success has perhaps been best argued by Theodore Schultz (1975). He suggests that entrepreneurs exist in an environment that is characterized by change, and the payoffs for such entrepreneurs are largely determined by whether they are capable of undertaking actions that will appropriately reallocate their resources to cope with changing circumstances. The central thesis is that the ability of the entrepreneur to deal with disequilibria efficiently is determined by her stock of human capital, especially in terms of education and experience. The likelihood that an entrepreneur will succeed in her optimizing behavior as she reallocates resources to regain equilibrium is largely dependent on the reserve of human capital she possesses.

Social capital constraints: Immigrant entrepreneurs in the United States often perceive the social context of a "foreign land" to be a constraint in their search for capital. Some individuals, for example, fear being discriminated against by bankers and are hesitant to approach them with loan requests. Lack of access to the broader social network prevents many minority entrepreneurs from accessing information on loan sources. At other times, lack of support among family and friends prevents access to informal finance.

The notion that an entrepreneur's ability to access capital is related to a community's social capital is rooted in the network theory of entrepreneurship. This theory suggests that an individual's social context is a key determinant of entrepreneurial success (Birley, 1987). Community networks can foster entrepreneurship by playing two key roles. First, social forces, such as those found in ethnic enclaves, lead to higher densities of networks that are capable of collective action and resource pooling. For instance, past familiarity and reputation mechanisms often allow co-ethnics to screen out bad credit risks and to assist each other. According to Aldrich and Zimmer (1985):

> Strong ties carry with them a history of past dealings in or out of a business setting that can form a basis for trust. Whereas banks and other formal institutions outside an ethnic group may have little or no objective credit history for an aspiring entrepreneur, within the group strong ties keep alive the memory of past experiences from which to infer trustworthiness, and these relationships may carry strong expectations of trust. (p. 15)

Second, social networks often allow for the flow of information through individuals or organizations that act as information-brokers at low transaction costs. These can include educational institutions, political advocacy agencies, community-based programs, and religious organizations. These entities often have access to key information about sources of capital and business resources and serve an important social role in enterprise development.

Indeed, where social capital reserves are high, communities may be more likely to be able to access capital from informal sources and, as a result, succeed in entrepreneurship (Light, 1972; Light and Bonacich, 1988; Waldinger, 1995).[6] The source of social capital can lie within the family or within kinship networks that exist in ethnic enclaves such as those established by Korean entrepreneurs in Los Angeles and Chinese entrepreneurs in New York (Light and Bonacich, 1988; Sanders and Nee, 1996; Waldinger, 1986).

The success of the self-employed Japanese American maintenance gardeners in Southern California provides an example of how ethnic solidarity can play a key role in microenterprise development. Although the gardeners operated their businesses independently, they did not function as isolated entrepreneurs. As in the larger Japanese community, their small businessmen were tied to a network of kin affiliations. These ties resulted not only in the social organization of the community but also in making it economically self-sufficient.

> Of special importance were the economic benefits. One of them was the *tanomoshi* or rotating-credit association. This provincial arrangement was an important source of capital for small businesses. Because collateral and formal contracts were replaced with trust, loans became easier and cheaper to acquire than negotiating with formal lending institutions. That members were often from the same prefecture, resided in the same district of the host society, and were employed in the same trade augmented its utility. (Tsukashima, 1991, p. 344)

That social capital—defined in terms of trustworthy relationships and informational networks that are characterized by ethnic solidarity and reciprocity—can be a key determinant of the level of a community's economic development has gained much recognition in the United States, especially due to the influential work of Robert Putnam.[7] In what was perhaps the first longitudinal study of the impact of social capital, Putnam's (1993a) research on the economic development of northern and southern Italy found support for the hypothesis that greater reserves of social capital are associated with higher levels of economic development.

His conclusions are also reflected in the essay, "The Prosperous Community," which argues that erosion of social capital in the America's inner cities is key to explaining its poverty and state of underdevelopment. "Part of the problem facing blacks and Latinos in the inner city is that they lack 'connections' in the most literal sense." He argues that when such networks and connections exist, "like conventional capital for conventional borrowers, social capital serves as a kind of collateral for men and women who are excluded from ordinary credit . . . markets" (Putnam, 1993b, p. 40).

ANALYZING CONSTRAINTS TO ENTERPRISE DEVELOPMENT

In order to investigate factors that constrain microenterprise development, we conducted a study of 103 entrepreneurs in the California area who had been declined bank financing (see appendix for research methodology).

Tables 3.3 and 3.4 provide a description of the socioeconomic characteristics of the entrepreneurs surveyed. Figure 3.1 and table 3.5 present the results of the data analysis. As shown in figure 3.1, the lack of working capital was perceived to be the more important capital constraint, with an average rating of 3.13, followed by lack of capital for equipment, with an average rating of 3.12. The lack of management skills was perceived to be the next most important factor with a factor rating of 2.87. Lack of sales and information followed, with factor ratings of 2.69 and 2.63 respectively.

Next, the data were analyzed to study how perceptions of each of the above constraints varied with the entrepreneur's gender, education, and ethnicity. As shown in table 3.5, the reported working capital constraint was not significantly related to any of the independent variables. Lack of capital for equipment, however, was perceived as a constraint among Hispanic entrepreneurs at the 0.1 level of statistical significance.

Table 3.3. Socioeconomic characteristics of microentrepreneurs surveyed in California (discrete variables)

Characteristics	Value	Frequency	Percentage
Gender	Female	62	60.19
	Male	41	39.81
Ethnicity	African American	41	39.81
	Caucasian	26	25.24
	Asian	19	18.45
	Hispanic	·17	16.50
Marital status	Married	41	39.81
	Single	34	33.01
	Divorced	26	25.24
	Widowed	2	1.94
Business status	Existing	69	66.99
	Start-up	34	33.01
Personal savings account?	Yes	35	33.98
	No	68	66.01
Financial condition better than parents?	Yes	54	52.43
	No	49	47.57

N=103

Table 3.4. Socioeconomic characteristics of microentrepreneurs surveyed in California (continuous variables)

CHARACTERISTICS	MEAN	STANDARD DEVIATION
Age	42.75	10.49
Years of education	13.69	3.59
Years in business	4.56	4.56
Number of people in household	2.86	1.79
Household income/month	$2,567.93	$2,109.66
Start-up capital	$3,638.15	$5,261.65

N=103

Figure 3.1. Perceived constraints to enterprise development identified during survey of microentrepreneurs in California

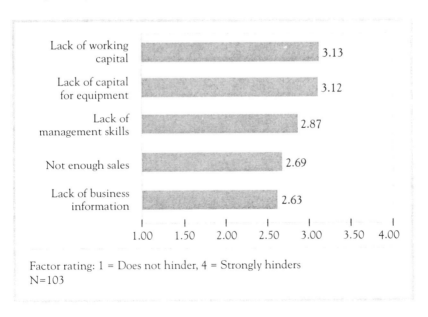

Factor rating: 1 = Does not hinder, 4 = Strongly hinders
N=103

Table 3.5. Some determinants of perceived constraints to enterprise development identified during survey of microentrepreneurs in California

VARIABLES	CAPITAL FOR INVENTORY	CAPITAL FOR EQUIPMENT	INFORMATION	SALES	MANAGEMENT SKILLS
Gender	0.0715	−0.0945	0.2843	0.1951	0.1734
	(0.27)	(−0.35)	(1.13)	(0.79)	(0.66)
Education	−0.0021	0.0007	0.0036	0.0383	0.1733[b]
	(−0.06)	(0.02)	(0.11)	(1.22)	(2.19)
Ethnicity					
Caucasian	0.4753	1.0661	−0.5170	0.4771	0.6356
	(0.55)	(1.24)	(−0.64)	(0.59)	(0.74)
African American	−0.2846	0.1194	−0.8835	0.5222	0.5377
	(−0.34)	(0.14)	(−1.12)	(0.67)	(0.64)
Asian	0.5743	0.9645	−0.6428	0.8263	0.7261
	(0.65)	(1.07)	(−0.76)	(0.99)	(0.82)
Hispanic	0.8991	1.4612[a]	−0.1135	1.5897[b]	1.5734[a]
	(1.03)	(1.64)	(−0.14)	(1.93)	(1.79)

[a] Significant at the 0.1 level
[b] Significant at the 0.05 level
Note: t-values are provided in parentheses.

None of the independent variables seemed to have any significant impact on the constraint related to lack of business information. The lack of sales, however, was most pronounced among Hispanic entrepreneurs, at the 0.05 level of statistical significance. Similarly, lack of management skills was significantly and positively related to the entrepreneur's education at the 0.05 level. The constraint was most pronounced among Hispanic entrepreneurs and was statistically significant at the 0.1 level.

Discussion: The results indicate that the entrepreneurs felt constrained in accessing capital for such purposes as equipment purchase. The regression analysis suggests that this was especially pronounced among the Hispanic entrepreneurs.

Although focus group participants from Caucasian and Asian communities had approached family and friends for loans, those from African American and Hispanic groups had not done so. Participants from these groups stated that they did not feel "comfortable" asking others for money, especially because their relatives and friends were themselves having a hard time making ends meet. While the Asian entrepreneurs had been successful in borrowing money from their families, the Caucasian entrepreneurs in the focus groups said that they had already approached their family or friends at the time of business start-up, and that they did not want to go back to the same "sources" again.

None of the entrepreneurs had previously worked in their areas of business, and all them had been refused bank loans. But half of them did not think that this constrained their ability to develop their businesses. Six Asian start-up entrepreneurs were able to obtain financing from their families to buy equipment, while another two Caucasian entrepreneurs, who were apparel designers, were able to obtain credit from their suppliers for buying fabric. Out of the six Asian entrepreneurs, however, four were on the verge of closing down their businesses because they could not generate enough revenue, while the remaining two, who were garment contractors and had bought sewing machines, were struggling for customers and jobs. It is not surprising that banks would have turned down requests from these entrepreneurs. Financing fixed assets is a risky proposition when an entrepreneur has had little experience in the line of business and when the asset cannot be put to use to generate income.

Although the results suggest that individuals faced barriers in raising capital from formal and informal sources, our interviews with the above entrepreneurs raise doubts about the extent to which their stated "credit needs" constrained their ability to develop microenterprises. The individuals seemed to lack the capacity to handle debt, and the inadequacy of the cash flow from their businesses suggests that they were poor credit risks, which is probably why banks refused to extend them loans.

A second factor that reportedly constrained the entrepreneurs was the lack of management skills. Regression analysis suggested that the constraint was most pronounced among Hispanic entrepreneurs. Further, it increased with the level of educational attainment, suggesting that entrepreneurs with higher education felt that they lacked the skills for successfully managing their enterprises. Although this finding seems surprising at first, especially since one would expect higher levels of education to serve as a proxy for greater human capital, it is consistent with the results of Stuart and Abetti's (1986) study, which found a negative relationship between firm success and the entrepreneur's educational level.

The role of formal education in enhancing chances of enterprise development has been questioned by several observers. According to Cooper and Gascon (1992), for instance, "it is not clear whether the things which are learned in school are enough to achieve success. Commitment and determination, obsession with opportunities, and tolerance for ambiguity may be critical . . .

yet these may not be the product of formal education" (p. 306). Grenell (1998), on the other hand, is more affirmative, arguing that traditional education "is a barrier toward developing entrepreneurs who have the right stuff" (p. 345). This is because entrepreneurs acquire human capital not so much by formal schooling as by informal processes such as previous management experiences and interaction with customers and competitors on the one hand, and through informal education acquired by attending entrepreneurial and technical training courses on the other (Day, 1992; Grenell, 1998).

The focus group interviews revealed additional information on the human capital of the entrepreneurs. Most individuals were not able to assess the viability of their business ideas. A number of entrepreneurs stated that they had mistakenly equated the creation of a product/service with the existence of a market for it. Since they did not possess the skills and tools that could help them analyze if their business start-up or growth idea was feasible, some of them had channeled their energies into developing nonviable enterprises. As a result, many were struggling to "keep afloat."

For microcredit programs that provide loans to entrepreneurs to start or grow ventures, the determination of business feasibility is extremely important. Specifically, in instances where markets are either saturated or lacking, an initial feasibility study can serve as a warning and prevent the launch of a venture that is likely to fail. Individuals with start-up ventures can also benefit from general business planning classes, although existing entrepreneurs engaged in income-generating activities are less likely to need this training. A couple of hours of technical assistance, for example, is often sufficient to assess the viability of an existing entrepreneur's plans for business expansion. Given that different entrepreneurs may be at different stages of venture creation and growth, and as a result may face different challenges, programs need to carefully select their target clients and conduct accurate assessments of their entrepreneurial capacity and educational needs.

Another factor constraining the development of the entrepreneurs' ventures was the lack of sales. The constraint was most pronounced among Hispanic entrepreneurs. Lack of sales suggests either the lack of appropriate customer targeting or the lack of a market itself. Although most programs assist entrepreneurs in the former area, that is, in developing advertising and promotional strategies, most such plans are theoretical. They assume that a customer base exists for an entrepreneur's goods or services and that "reaching" the customer is the critical challenge. But many of the products and services offered by microentrepreneurs do not have ready markets. Indeed, during the focus group interviews, most entrepreneurs complained about the "lack of revenues" being a major business problem.

This is an area that has traditionally received little attention by many program designers, who have assumed that the provision of capital and generic training will enable entrepreneurs to succeed. Specifically, many programs are often so moved by potential borrowers' past hardships and present motivation to control their own destinies that they fail to thoroughly evaluate whether their business ideas have any potential in the marketplace. Many of these initiatives follow the philosophy of some Third World microlenders that the entrepreneur has intimate knowledge of the marketplace and can invest in activities with the highest potential return.

But in those Third World countries where microcredit programs have been most successful, the absorptive capacity of informal markets is immense. Formal markets are underdeveloped. Often, they do not offer the wide array of cheap goods and service alternatives that the informal sector entrepreneurs can provide. Due to its buying power and convenience, the informal sector economizes for both the entrepreneurs and customers.

Peru's informal sector, for example, generates more than 60 percent of the country's GDP, and more than 50 percent of the population is engaged in informal sector entrepreneurship. Barriers to generating income in markets are quite low. The huge market demand, especially for the food products that a large number of vendors sell, makes such ventures economically worthwhile for many low-income entrepreneurs. As a result "gross sales are considerable: $6.2 million a week, or roughly $322.2 million a year. . . . For every $100 in sales, they net a profit of $18.30; . . . the net per capita income from street vending (is) 38 percent more than the legal minimum wage" (de Soto, 1989, pp. 60–61).

ANALYSIS OF CONSTRAINTS TO CAPITAL ACCESS

Figure 3.2 and table 3.6 present the results of the data analysis. As shown in figure 3.2 in their order of importance—lack of collateral, inadequate business profitability, and credit problems were respectively reported as the key constraints to accessing capital (factor ratings 3.04, 2.96, and 2.91 respectively). These were followed by lack of planning, lack of information on loans, and lack of management skills (factor ratings 2.90, 2.87, and 2.83 respectively).

Next, the data were analyzed to study how perceptions of each of the above nine constraints varied with the entrepreneur's gender, education, and ethnicity (see table 3.6). Problems with credit history constrained African American entrepreneurs, as well as Hispanic and Asian entrepreneurs (significant at the 0.1 level). Lack of collateral was most constraining to African American entrepreneurs.

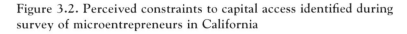

Figure 3.2. Perceived constraints to capital access identified during survey of microentrepreneurs in California

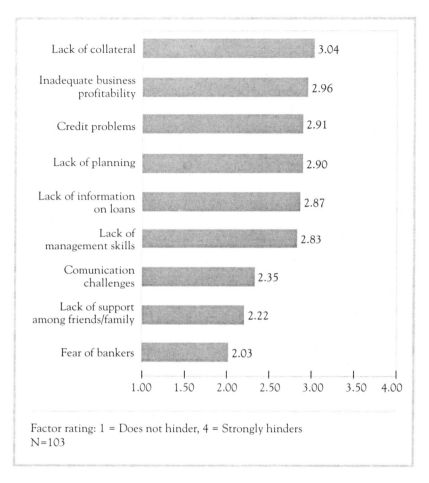

Factor rating: 1 = Does not hinder, 4 = Strongly hinders
N=103

Lack of profits, as well as the lack of business planning skills, were significantly and positively related to the probability of an entrepreneur being female. Problems related to inadequate communication skills, as well as lack of business management skills, were significantly and negatively related to the educational level of the entrepreneur. Finally, while the reluctance to approach

Table 3.6. Some determinants of perceived constraints to capital access identified during survey of microentrepreneurs in California

Independent Variables	Credit Problems	Collateral Problems	Profitability Problems	Planning Problems	Communication Problems	Management Problems	Fear of Bankers	Lack of Information	Lack of Support
Gender	0.3553 (-1.46)	-0.0078 (-0.03)	0.4569[a] (2.07)	0.3883[a] (1.72)	0.2461 (-1.14)	-0.1936 (-0.74)	0.1091 (0.45)	0.1129 (0.41)	0.0382 (0.14)
Education	0.0009 (0.30)	-0.0272 (-0.93)	-0.0467[a] (-1.66)	-0.0174 (-0.60)	-0.0834[c] (-3.03)	-0.0638[b] (-1.91)	-0.0423 (-1.39)	-0.0293 (-0.85)	-0.0159 (-0.47)
Ethnicity									
Caucasian	0.7738 (0.99)	0.4323 (0.59)	-0.5639 (-0.79)	-1.1433 (-1.58)	-1.2436[a] (-1.79)	0.1388 (0.16)	0.1317 (0.77)	0.1754 (0.20)	-0.0891 (0.11)
African American	1.6321[b] (2.13)	1.2679[a] (1.74)	0.3591 (0.52)	-0.9927 (-1.39)	-1.0141 (-1.49)	0.1481 (0.178)	0.6804 (0.75)	-0.5357 (-0.62)	0.5975[a] (1.71)
Asian	1.3916[a] (1.71)	1.1586 (1.51)	0.4943 (0.67)	-1.1243 (-1.48)	0.1667 (0.23)	-0.1566 (-0.178)	1.2309 (0.80)	-0.2028 (-0.22)	1.3383 (1.54)
Hispanic	1.5014[a] (1.86)	1.2173 (1.56)	-0.1454 (-0.19)	-0.9514 (-1.27)	-0.0768 (-0.12)	0.3875 (0.44)	1.0298 (1.21)	0.7006 (0.77)	-0.9121 (-1.04)

[a] Significant at the 0.1 level
[b] Significant at the 0.05 level
[c] Significant at the 0.005 level
Note: t-values are provided in parentheses.

bankers and the lack of information were not statistically significant, the lack of support from family and friends was significantly and positively related to the probability of an entrepreneur being African American.

Discussion: These results, when combined with entrepreneurs' comments during the focus group sessions, suggest that individuals felt capital constrained mainly because of the stringent underwriting criteria employed by banks. The lack of collateral, inadequate business profitability, and credit problems were the major reasons these entrepreneurs were turned down for loans.

When one compares the above perceptions of loan applicants with those of conventional credit suppliers, as documented by Dymski and Veitch (1991), there seems to be a close consistency. In their survey of 36 Los Angeles area banks, the authors constructed a three-point scale (0=seldom, 3=often), asking lenders to rate on this scale each of nine different reasons for small-business loan denials. The study suggested that factors related to a borrower's collateral, credit, and business profitability were paramount.

For instance, Dymski and Veitch (1991) found that the financial institutions required, on average, 87.4 percent of the loan amount as collateral, and reported that insufficient borrower collateral was one of the key reasons that credit was denied (factor rating of about 2.3). A second important reason for loan denial was the credit history of the owner (factor rating 2.2). Finally, the third top reason for loan denial was applicants' high debt-to-income ratios (factor rating 2.6). This seems to be consistent with the perceptions of the entrepreneurs surveyed in this study, who identified inadequacy of business profits as key to their inability to access bank credit. At given levels of debt, low levels of profitability can often mean low levels of income for the entrepreneur,[8] which can lead to high debt-to-income ratios.

Our analysis suggests that credit and collateral problems created significant barriers for some African American and Hispanic entrepreneurs. This finding seems to be consistent with Goldsmith and Blakely's (1992) finding that these two minority communities are severely disadvantaged with regard to their credit histories and asset holdings. Indeed, out of the 35 survey respondents who reported not having a personal savings account, 26 belonged to these two ethnic groups.

Insufficient reserves of human capital were also perceived to create barriers in the entrepreneurs' ability to access capital. Since many microentrepreneurs do not have access to traditional financing, they need to rely on "creative" sources to finance their business.[9] Alternative financing mechanisms may include supplier credit, customer advances, and collaborative partnerships with other entrepreneurs to share property, plant, and equipment. But the ability to structure such deals depends heavily on the management skills possessed by the entrepreneur. Our analysis indicates that once again, Hispanic and African American entrepreneurs feel constrained due to the lack of such skills.[10]

Finally, although the lack of confidence in bankers, information, and support among family and friends also constrained access to capital, these factors seemed to matter more for entrepreneurs belonging to certain ethnic groups. Specifically, the interviews with African American entrepreneurs indicated that they lacked access to information regarding capital sources and were not successful in obtaining financing from informal sources such as family and friends. This might have been due to the lack of support networks, a factor that was found to be statistically significant in the regression analysis. This finding is consistent with Putnam's (1993b) argument that African American entrepreneurs are unable to access informal financing due to the low reserves of social capital in their communities.

Although the fear of bankers was found to be statistically insignificant, the Asian and Hispanic entrepreneurs mentioned that this fear was widespread in their communities. To the extent that this might be true, it suggests that segments of minority entrepreneurs might not be approaching lenders at all with requests for loans. There might be some within such a segment who are creditworthy, or are close to being so, and yet cannot access institutional assistance owing to the fear of being excluded from what are perceived as "closed" social and business networks (Coleman, 1988, 1993). Microcredit programs need to allay the fears of such individuals by engaging in targeted outreach, preferably in Spanish or Asian languages, through community-based organizations. Only by reaching out to include the historically excluded minority and immigrant communities can lending institutions create trust and social capital, which in turn can increase "deal-flow." In doing so, however, it is important to recognize that because "social capital is not a substitute for effective public policy but rather a prerequisite for it," such outreach needs to be complemented with business development services that analyze the market feasibility of proposed start-up or expansion proposals (Putnam, 1993b, p. 42).

IMPLICATIONS

Although the lack of capital might be perceived to be an important constraint to enterprise development, it is nonfinancial factors, especially low levels of revenues and profits, that seem to create significant barriers for microentrepreneurs in the United States. While policy makers have cited credit market failures to emulate Third World programs and offer unsecured loans to individuals with poor credit histories, they have paid less attention to perhaps the most important factor making programs successful overseas: successful lenders make loans only to those who have adequate debt capacity. For start-up entrepreneurs, for example, lending decisions are based on the existing, not just projected, cash flows of the borrower and her household. For existing entrepreneurs, a borrower's business potential and credit record are checked by loan agents who solicit this information from suppliers, customers, neighbors, and moneylenders. In most instances, however, although loans can be used to generate sales almost immediately, lenders assess an individual's cash inflows and debt service capacity not only from project revenues, but also from the borrower's total household income, which can result from other self-employment and/or wage employment activities of the borrower and her family members. This is done to ensure that the lender will be repaid even if a borrower's business fails.

Microentrepreneurs in the United States can seldom provide lenders with such security. Unlike in the Third World, many small-scale entrepreneurs do not have income-generating ventures or family members whose income can be "secured" to service the debt should the borrower be unwilling or unable to do so. While it may be true that some conventional banks in the United States practice "lending discrimination," the low levels of business revenues and profitability among microenterprises suggest that this behavior might be rational. Approving loan requests in the absence of *all* of the following factors—good credit history, collateral, cash flow, and capacity (indicated by the borrower's entrepreneurship skills and experiences)—defies the very fundamentals of prudent underwriting. In addition to being cost ineffective, it is also highly risky.

But while advocates and program designers may theoretically appreciate the importance of each of the above factors in alleviating risk, many often fail to translate these "first principles" into practice. For example, most programs offer general entrepreneurship classes and loans based on the *a priori* assumption that it is the lack of entrepreneurship capacity and capital that constrains enterprise development. But classes and capital by themselves do not make microentrepreneurs viable—it is markets for desired goods and services that ultimately generate revenues and profits. Since few programs assist individuals on a one-on-one basis to specifically develop businesses that have ready market potential, most entrepreneurs, especially those in the start-up stages, struggle just to pay the bills, even before they can think about making loan repayments or taking an owner's draw. Many such ventures launched in unfavorable market environments face a slow and often painful demise, harming the entrepreneur who invests time, energy, and hope in developing the business, as well as the microcredit program, which usually invests public funds to support the training and lending activities.

Ultimately, making entrepreneurs out of people with few resources is a matter not only of increasing the supply of capital but also nourishing the demand for it. In this regard, policies and programs that provide microentrepreneurs with access to markets might be as critical, if not more important, than those that build their human capital.

NOTES

1. It is perhaps due to their nonviability that 60 percent of new businesses fail within two years. For statistics on business failure rates in the United States, see Bracker (1993, p. 303).

2. Individual Development Accounts (IDAs) provide incentives to the poor to save by providing matching funds—up to four times the amount put in by an individual. Public and private sector entities are encouraged to match deposits for low-income families and to participate in providing the financial literacy training that often accompanies these programs. The matched savings can be used for such purposes as homeownership, education, job training, and small-business development.

As of January 2000, 27 states had passed IDA legislation, and more than 200 community-based IDA programs had been implemented around the country. Recent welfare-to-work grants to community-based agencies have recommended integration of IDA initiatives with microenterprise development programs. This strategy to induce savings, however, has not yet been incorporated by many programs and thus is limited in scale.

The theoretical development of IDA concepts is credited to the pioneering work of Michael Sherraden (1991). The Corporation of Enterprise Development has taken the lead in translating these principles into federal and state policies and community-based programs.

3. In general, lack of sales can result from at least three distinct yet related factors: (i) the inability of the entrepreneur to employ appropriate tactics to correctly identify and reach customers; (ii) the lack of a market; and (iii) the presence of a number of other players in the market, many of whom offer better value to the customers in cost, quality, and convenience. While sales problems due to the first factor are usually related to the lack of appropriate customer targeting and inappropriate promotional strategies, a number of small-scale entrepreneurs face problems because of the second and third factors, which are considered here.

4. This is especially argued by those who believe *strictly* in the conception of an entrepreneur as presented by Schumpeter (1934). He saw the entrepreneur as an innovator who creates new combinations of economic development, which are new goods, new methods of production, new markets, new sources of raw material, or new organizational forms. According to him, in creating new combinations, such an entrepreneur generates profits. Critics argue that most small-scale activities do not result in such new combinations and hence should not be thought of as being entrepreneurial. In fact, some scholars insist that not all small-business owners are entrepreneurs. The Schumpeterian concept of entrepreneurship and economic development is discussed extensively by Barreto (1989).

5. Other factors not considered in the study, but also important from a lender's perspective are (1) the amount of capital contributed by the entrepreneur toward the project for which the loan is being sought, and (2) the debt-to-income ratio of the borrowing entity.

6. Some scholars have suggested that the economic advantages of ethnic networks are limited to the start-up phases of a venture. For example,

in his study of Eastern European immigrants in Pennsylvania, Rothbart (1993) concludes that ethnic entrepreneurship had little positive impact on the advancement of entrepreneurs. According to him, only those entrepreneurs "who diversified or expanded beyond the ethnic saloon market accumulated wealth." Similarly, in his investigations of several Asian immigrant groups, Bates (1994) found that reliance on social support networks was associated with lower profits and high venture failure rates.

7. For example, a 1995 report of a hearing before the Committee on Small Business in the United States Senate has an entire chapter devoted to this issue (U.S. Government Printing Office, 1995).

8. We assume that the entrepreneur takes a draw after covering all expenses.

9. Bracker (1993), citing research conducted by the National Federation of Independent Business, reports that only 23 percent of all the entrepreneurs who start businesses that were previously nonexistent are able to access financing from traditional lending institutions. Nearly 70 percent of the financing is acquired from personal funds and friends and family.

10. The latter might seem to be a surprising finding, since in the first part of our survey it was the entrepreneurs with higher levels of education who reported being managerially constrained. But a deeper analysis reveals why this might have been the case. In the first part of the survey, entrepreneurs were asked to focus on factors they thought were important to the growth and development of their enterprises, and their responses suggest that lack of management acumen was perceived to hinder firm growth. In the second part of the survey, however, the focus was on the acquisition of capital and the extent to which management skills impeded such a process. It is possible that in the first part of the survey, entrepreneurs with higher levels of education who were finding it difficult to grow their businesses might have thought that it reflected an inadequacy in terms of their management skills, and that in the second part of the survey, these entrepreneurs, to the extent that they were successful in acquiring capital, might have felt that it was their superior business management acumen that accounted for their ability to capitalize their business. In other words, it seems that while entrepreneurs with higher levels of education may successfully search for and acquire capital, they may not be as successful in developing and growing their enterprises upon capitalization.

CHAPTER FOUR

Loan Repayment Performance

The viability of microcredit programs depends to a large extent on their ability to collect in a timely fashion the principal and interest that is owed to them by borrowers. This is because when loan payments are late, interest income is postponed. Further, when loans are not paid back at all, a program loses the principal as well as interest income. In both instances, since the total value of the funds available for future lending is diminished, the speed with which the portfolio can be revolved slows down, adversely impacting fees and interest income that could have been generated by making additional loans.

Both the programs and clients suffer due to these portfolio problems (Christen, 1997). For example, because delinquent accounts[1] require above-average monitoring and maintenance, they consume staff time and resources and increase administrative expenses.[2] A decrease in revenues and an increase in costs reduce a program's cash flow, resulting in a shortfall of funds to cover day-to-day operating expenses. Further, a program that is unable to collect timely repayments needs a larger loan loss reserve.[3] Since provisions for loan losses need to be regularly expensed from a program's income statement, program earnings decrease as provisioning requirements increase. In addition to these program-level challenges, poor loan repayment performance also impacts clients adversely, since fewer funds for lending mean that current and future entrepreneurs who want to borrow at a later date might not be able to do so.

Given the importance of maintaining timely loan repayments, accurately assessing and managing the risks associated with lending become extremely critical to a program's survival. One dimension of reducing credit risk is to lend only to those applicants who have adequate debt capacity, which, as discussed in chapter 3, is indicated by their current personal and project cash flows. Another aspect, one that is especially important in the absence of legal guarantees, is accurately assessing the willingness of borrowers to keep their promises and repay their loans per terms and timetables that were originally agreed upon. In other words, the ability of lending institutions to screen out individuals who will be either unable or unwilling to repay is fundamental to their viability. In this regard, designing incentives and sanctioning mechanisms that make loan repayment beneficial and default costly for borrowers is extremely important. Successful programs in Third World countries have created such loan delivery systems, and they have been quite effective in addressing the above problems of adverse selection and moral hazard. According to Christen (1997), for instance,

Microfinance as we now know it began in the early 1970s. By the end of the first decade, pioneer work done by the

Grameen Bank in Bangladesh and ACCION International in Latin America had developed a variety of methodologies that achieved sustained loan repayment rates of about 95%. Up until then, not only bankers but also most development credit practitioners believed that poor clients represent a very high credit risk. . . . Modern microenterprise credit programs [demonstrated] that repayment depends fundamentally on factors within the control of the lending institution, such as reliability and quality of loan service, communication of clear repayment expectations, administrative efficiency, and the development of a close, almost personal, relationship with clients. . . . In lending to poor clients, selection of borrowers and enforcement of timely repayment are problematic. The informal nature of clients' enterprises and the character of their capital assets make traditional lending techniques nearly worthless for both purposes. . . . Successful microcredit programs base much of their risk assessment on prior credit performance, starting new clients off with small, low-risk loans and then moving them up into larger loans as borrowers demonstrate their capacity and willingness to repay. (p. 16)

This chapter examines the extent to which Third World microcredit replications in the United States have succeeded in reducing credit risk. First we discuss typical risk-reduction mechanisms associated with microenterprise lending. This is followed by a brief description of the four programs selected for our empirical study. Next we develop and test hypotheses to assess the individual and institutional determinants of loan repayment in these programs. Finally, we present the implications of our findings for designing microcredit programs.

RISK REDUCTION IN MICROENTERPRISE LENDING

Efficient credit transactions depend largely on the ability of transacting parties—lenders and borrowers—to reduce the risks they need to bear (Stiglitz, 1987; Von Pischke, 1991). Various institutions in credit markets differ in their methods for risk reduction.

Informal credit and moneylenders: In informal credit markets, lenders are seldom interested in the kind of project for which a loan is requested. Instead, they estimate the risk of a loan by their personal knowledge about the potential borrower's reputation in the community and past loan repayment behavior (Von Pischke, 1991). The moneylending trade is viable in many settings because both lenders and borrowers are able to save on transaction costs. Borrowers can save time and other costs they need to incur if they attempt to borrow from the formal banking sector. Lenders can economize on the costs associated with project or collateral appraisal, contract monitoring, and time-consuming collection procedures. Moneylenders and their operations have by and large stood the test of time and remained an important, and in many areas the only, source of credit for low-income communities around the world.

Despite its ability to economize on transaction costs and alleviate risk for the lender, the moneylending trade in U.S. inner-city communities suffers from many limitations. For example, Dymski and Veitch (1996) have described the limitations of what they refer to as "corner store finance" in the Los Angeles area thus:

> . . . communities turn to this growing second-tier financial sector to meet their financial needs. Check cashing outlets

and money orders are used for cash transactions and payments. These facilities are widely available to even the poorest households, for a price. Generally, the cost of these transactions varies inversely with the household's economic status. For obtaining credit, the options are fewer. Pawnbrokers have been described as the short-term credit market for the poor, but this is overly generous. . . . They offer credit on terms more onerous than those of the formal sector. Bank credit facilitates the accumulation of new human and physical assets that enhance future income; in contrast, pawnbroker credit involves households' deaccumulation of their stock of assets to meet current income crises. (p. 49)

In addition to these limitations, the moneylending trade can also suffer from many abuses. For instance, in the event that borrowers are unable to repay the loan due to an unexpected economic shock or project failure, moneylenders have been known to resort to extreme and often inhumane methods to recover loans. In some places, such practices even entail physical injury. Considering such potential abuses and the trade's inability to provide a full spectrum of services, especially in terms of providing human capital–building services to the poor, a number of microcredit programs supported by various foundations, as well as public and private entities, have evolved. These programs have adopted both individual- and group-based lending methodologies.

Microcredit programs for individual borrowers: A number of programs across the United States have implemented individual lending methodologies with the objective of providing "credit to individuals who are marginalized from traditional sources, but are capable of developing and managing their businesses with relatively minimal support" (Edgcomb et al., 1996, p. 12). Such programs assume greater risk compared to traditional banks, given that their borrowers are often undercollateralized, have poor credit, lack appropriate management skills, and cannot formulate a workable business plan.

Despite its simplicity and close resemblance to the individual credit delivery system that is employed by traditional banks, this lending mechanism has proven to be resource intensive. This is because the transaction costs of making small loans are very high. Further, in most cases, providing business management and other technical assistance to borrowers is both costly and time consuming, especially for start-up entrepreneurs. Finally, many low-income individuals do not fit programs' "eligibility" criteria, which might require loan applicants to post some collateral or demonstrate business profitability. As a result, many low-income individuals are provided not individual, but group-based credit.

Microcredit programs for group borrowers: Group lending is a formal credit delivery innovation that, in its "ideal" form, relies on informal social relationships to reduce risk and transaction costs for both lenders and borrowers, thus capturing the major advantage of informal credit markets (Bhatt and Tang, 1998a). Microcredit programs in the United States adopted this methodology due to its success in achieving high loan repayment rates in Latin America and Asia. The founder of Bangladesh's Grameen Bank, Muhammad Yunus, explains the logic and design of group-based microcredit programs thus:

> When a person wanted to borrow from the Grameen Bank, we would ask her to form a group of five people. It is not an easy process. It takes time to find four other friends who would like to join with you. After you have successfully found four other friends, formed the group, then the bank would like to discuss with you the rules and procedures of

Grameen Bank. Among many things, the bank will explain that we will not give loans to all five at the same time. You choose two among yourselves, and preferably the most needy two, and we will give loans to these two persons first. And the group will be asked to watch out that they use the money right and the repayment is right, so that they don't get into any problems. Because if they get into problems in repayment, then we will have doubts about the group, we'll be hesitant to deal with the group in the future, meaning that the rest of the three may not receive their loans. Because of this, a kind of group support builds up. They help each other to overcome individual problems. You're not responsible only to yourself, now there is a sense of being responsible for others. When you are part of a group, you try and do things which will make everybody a winner . . . you want to do something together that your friends outside your group will appreciate. (Yunus, 1991, p. 27)

In principle, group lending enables the lending agency to deal with the credit group as an entity, saving the agency the costs of transacting with several different individuals. The lender thus *shifts* some transaction burdens to prospective borrowers by having them self-select group members based on reputation and familiarity in business and personal contexts. The intent is to lend money to groups whose members can internalize the otherwise high transaction costs associated with loan-disbursement activities. Intimate knowledge of each other's activities facilitates mutual monitoring, and the joint-liability principle creates peer pressure for repayment. Such informal relationships, or social collateral, can provide the lender with a substitute for traditional tangible collateral (Besley and Coate, 1995). Thus the lending agency can achieve a similar vantage point as the money-lender has, enjoying low transaction costs and loan default risks.

But regardless of the type of lending strategy employed, there are two major types of factors that determine loan repayment performance in microcredit programs. For the present purposes, these are discussed under individual-level factors, which include the socioeconomic characteristics of the borrowers, and institutional-level factors, which include community- and program-level characteristics.

In the following sections, we use data from four microcredit programs—Neighborhood Entrepreneurship Program (NEP), Community Enterprise Program (CEP), First Chance (FC), and Women's Development Association (WDA)—to study the impact of individual- and institutional-level factors on repayment performance.

DESCRIPTION OF MICROCREDIT PROGRAMS

All the agencies selected for the study made joint-liability loans to group members in the absence of credit checks or collateral requirements between 1989 and 1996. This choice of programs allowed us to compare the performance of programs that tried to "replicate" Third World programs that disburse unsecured credit to borrower-groups with no formal credit history. While all programs formally adopted group lending, they served a diversity of clients and had different funding sources (see chapter 1 for a brief description of each program).

The four programs together provide a rich diversity of experiences in microlending while sharing certain common features. For example, the minimum loan size for all programs was $500, and in principle, upon successful repayment, borrowers could access loans of up to $10,000. But only a small fraction (12 percent) of all loans were made to repeat clients, and all loans disbursed were between $500 and $3,000. While three agencies charged 10 percent nominal interest and no fees on the loans, the fourth (FC) charged 14 percent and a 10 percent loan origination fee. Administrative processes were also different between and within agencies. At NEP, for example, a facilitator *assisted* the group formation process to varying degrees. Specifically, while in some instances the decision to be in the same group was made by the prospective borrowers, in others, a facilitator "formed" the groups. At CEP, however, the agency formed the groups and the borrowers often had no say in the matter. Further, the four programs had different policies for dealing with loan defaulters. At FC, loan balances that were not paid for six months were usually written off as "bad debt," without further legal action; at CEP, default cases were sometimes taken to small claims courts.

All four programs provided us with agency records that captured the socioeconomic characteristics and repayment records of individual borrowers. This data allowed us to examine how individual-level socioeconomic characteristics affect the borrowers' likelihood of repayment.[4] In addition, we surveyed borrowers from the only program that permitted us to do so, NEP. A part of the survey was designed to capture each borrower's view about the loan disbursement process, including such institutional variables as transaction costs incurred by the borrower in the process of getting loans, homogeneity of the group in which the borrower belonged, and the perceived threat of sanctions for nonrepayment.

A partial payment made by a borrower was counted as a loan loss in the analysis. The reason for doing so was twofold. First, most agencies did not have accurate information on the status of such "partial" repayments; therefore, calculating the fraction of the loans repaid was difficult. Program staff indicated that those in default usually made no more than a couple of monthly installments on loan terms that ranged from 18 to 24 months for the programs. Further, the agencies had written off loans with partial payments and had not made any effort to collect on the remaining balances for over a year. (The lack of internal controls was surprising; at least three of the four programs lacked the professional systems that one would expect to see within any serious lending organization.) Second, a partial payment indicated either the inability or unwillingness of peer borrowers to "make up" for the debts of the defaulter. Since such joint liability is thought to be critical to the success of overseas microcredit approaches, the decision to focus on total loan repayments was appropriate given the research objective of assessing the viability of replicating Third World programs.

INDIVIDUAL-LEVEL VARIABLES AND LOAN REPAYMENT

Hypotheses: We were able to collect systematic data from all four programs on six individual-level socioeconomic variables that have been hypothesized in the literature to be important determinants of loan repayment: (1) the borrower's gender; (2) the borrower's educational level; (3) the borrower's household income; (4) the degree of formality of the borrower's business; (5) the number of years that the borrower has been in business; and (6) the proximity of the borrower's business to the lending agency.

Gender: Low-income women are often victims of societal suppression in developing countries and victims of lending discrimination in developed countries (Bennett and Goldberg, 1993; Yunus, 1995; Rodriguez, 1995). Some argue that lending to women can lead to their economic empowerment,[5] and inculcate in them a culture of hard work and financial discipline, which in turn can lead to high loan repayment rates (Khandker et al., 1995). Thus women borrowers may have higher loan repayment rates.

Educational level: While many Third World microcredit borrowers have been able to maintain high repayment rates despite low educational levels, microentrepreneurs in the United States are faced with different circumstances. Unlike individuals in many developing countries who experience a ready market for their goods or services, microentrepreneurs in the United States often struggle to generate revenues. They are often unable to achieve returns on their investments that are high enough to allow them to cover operating costs and repay their loans. In some cases, this is due to their inability to produce goods or services that are in demand. In other cases, it is due to a lack of appropriate strategies for increasing internal efficiency and for effectively targeting customers. In this regard, compared with their counterparts in developing countries, some microentrepreneurs in the United States may need more formal education in order to comprehend complex information, keep business records, conduct basic cash flow analysis, and generally speaking, make the right business decisions (Bhatt et al., 1999b). Thus borrowers with higher levels of education may have higher repayment rates.

Household income: Microentrepreneurs often use their business loans for such household expenditures as paying for their children's education, buying food and supplies, and paying for medical bills and other emergency expenses (Clark and Kays, 1999). They may also use cash inflows from nonbusiness activities and sources—such as incomes from other jobs or incomes generated by other family members—to make loan repayments. Thus borrowers with higher household incomes may have a higher chance of repaying their loans.

Formality of business: Some microcredit programs seek to assist informal sector entrepreneurs such as street vendors and handyworkers who are often unlicensed and in some cases, undocumented immigrants. Membership in such poor communities often implies few alternatives for generating income and obtaining credit; consequently, microentrepreneurs in these communities are often eager to maintain a good credit history with the lending agency (Sirola, 1992). Thus, borrowers with less formal businesses, such as those without a business license, may have higher repayment rates.

Years in business: Microentrepreneurs who have been in business longer are expected to have more stable sales and cash flows than those who have just started. Thus, those who have run their businesses longer may have higher debt capacity.

Proximity of business to the lending agency: Many microentrepreneurs value convenience and flexibility in financial services more than they value the financial costs of accessing capital (Christen, 1992). Furthermore, if an entrepreneur's business is located close to the lender, it is easier for the lender to get information on the borrower and to provide her with appropriate technical assistance. Thus borrowers with businesses closer to the lending agency may have higher repayment rates.

In summary, six hypotheses can be specified as follows:

H1: Female borrowers have a higher chance of loan repayment.

H2: Borrowers with higher levels of education have a higher chance of loan repayment.

H3: Borrowers with higher household incomes have a higher chance of loan repayment.

H4: Borrowers without a business license have a higher chance of loan repayment.

H5: Borrowers with more business experience have a higher chance of loan repayment.

H6: Borrowers whose businesses are located closer to the lending agency have a higher chance of loan repayment.

A statistical test: A logit model is specified that consists of two probabilities associated with the dependent variable REPAY, with a value of 1 denoting loan repayment and 0 for loan default.

Table 4.1 provides definitions of the variables of interest. Table 4.2 includes descriptive statistics for each variable.[6] The results of estimating the logit model are presented in table 4.3. Two variables, EDUCATN and PROXMITY, are statistically significant at the 0.05 and 0.01 levels respectively. None of the other variables, including the interaction terms, are significant.

Table 4.1. Definition of individual-level variables for four microcredit programs that operated in California between 1989 and 1996

Variable	Description
REPAY	Whether a borrower repaid the loan at all
GENDER	Whether a borrower was male or female
EDUCATN	The level of formal education acquired by a borrower
HINCOME	The level of a borrower's total household income
LICENSE	The presence or absence of a business license
YRS_IN_B	The number of years an entrepreneur had been in the business
PROXMITY	Whether or not the entrepreneur's business was located in the same zip code as the lending agency

Table 4.2. Descriptive statistics for four microcredit programs that operated in California between 1989 and 1996

A. Aggregate loan repayment performance

SAMPLE CATEGORY	NUMBER OF BORROWERS	PERCENTAGE
Repayments	145	79
Losses	38	21
Total	183	100

B. Categorical independent variables

VARIABLE	VALUE	FREQUENCY	PERCENTAGE
Gender	Female	82	45
	Male	101	55
Business license	Yes	97	53
	No	86	47
Proximity	Yes	130	71
	No	53	29

N=183

C. Continuous dependent variables

VARIABLE	N	MEAN	STANDARD DEVIATION
Education (years)	183	11.34	3.11
Household income/month	174	$1381.39	$1340.51
Number of years in business	183	3.09	3.07

Discussion: The statistical results are both consistent and inconsistent with existing research on microcredit. That EDUCATN is significant in the statistical test is consistent with the entrepreneurship development literature. Entrepreneurs with higher educational levels tend to have more knowledge and skills in such areas as basic mathematics and accounting. Such human capital can assist entrepreneurs in better managing their businesses on a daily basis. Entrepreneurs with higher educational

Table 4.3. Logit model of repayment performance for four microcredit programs that operated in California between 1989 and 1996

Outcome variable REPAY=1, N= 174

VARIABLE	COEFFICIENT	WALD CHI-SQUARE	PROBABILITY VALUE
INTERCEPT	−3.92	6.96	0.008
GENDER	0.35	0.18	0.669
EDUCATN	0.23	6.12	0.013[a]
HINCOME	0.00	0.39	0.527
LICENSE	−0.11	0.03	0.858
YRS_IN_B	0.12	1.52	0.217
PROXMITY	2.38	13.89	0.002[b]
P1	0.88	1.09	0.294
P2	1.47	1.19	0.274
P3	−1.98	1.59	0.207
GENDER x P2	−1.19	0.91	0.338
HINCOME x P2	0.00	0.25	0.615
HINCOME x P3	0.00	1.03	0.311
LICENSE x P3	0.09	0.00	0.980
YRS_IN_B x P2	0.22	0.31	0.483
PROXMITY x P3	2.48	1.71	0.190
pseudo R^2	0.3141[c]		

[a] Significant at 0.05 level
[b] Significant at 0.01 level
[c] A number of pseudo R^2 measures have been proposed in the literature. The one employed here is from Aldrich and Nelson (1984).

levels may also find it easier to find part-time jobs to supplement their incomes. These supplemental incomes may help the borrowers to repay loans in the event of business failure.

That PROXMITY is significant in the statistical test is also consistent with previous microcredit research. The finding, for example, echoes the Grameen Bank's principle of "taking the bank to the people." Of course, none of the four programs engaged in the type of mobile banking available in some developing countries, where loan officers often transact at the borrower's doorstep.[7] Yet, being closer and spending less time commuting to the lender allows borrowers to put more time into running their businesses. Being closer also gives lenders more information about the day-to-day situation of borrowers more quickly, allowing them to provide the needed technical assistance to borrowers "in trouble." In any event, reducing transaction costs by being closer to the lender increases a borrower's chance of repayment.

The insignificance of the variable GENDER merits discussion, because microcredit has historically been thought of as a development intervention that addresses gender biases in credit markets, and thus works best with women borrowers. Specifically, women are believed to be better credit risks, because they see microcredit not only as a vehicle for generating incomes for personal uses but also for the use of the family, especially their children. Some observers have also suggested that women are more likely than men to assist and support one another should they experience financial difficulties (Bennett and Goldberg, 1993). This is especially important for group-lending programs, in which loan recovery depends in part on the willingness of group members to help each other out when they encounter project failures or other income shocks.

Given this reasoning, why did women in our four research programs not exhibit a higher propensity for loan repayment? One possible reason is that some women entrepreneurs, consistent with experiences elsewhere (Spalter-Roth et al., 1994), may have engaged in high-risk, low-return activities that undermined their ability to generate sufficient revenues and profits to repay their loans. This explanation is also supported by Goldsmith and Blakely's (1992) research which documented that self-employed women in the United States earn less than half as much as men.

Another possible reason is that low-income women in the United States have access to more public benefits than men of similar socioeconomic backgrounds. Following Mead's (1989) line of argument, the ready availability of government welfare programs may reduce the incentives for borrowers to ensure business success and loan repayment. The knowledge that a future source of income by way of public support is available may make default a rational choice over repayment, especially for those who have no experience in income-generating activities to begin with. Thus, unlike borrowers in some developing countries, where future credit is key to increasing earning ability or reducing future vulnerability (Morduch, 1998), women in this study might not have been that dependent on future credit as an income source.

INSTITUTIONAL VARIABLES AND LOAN REPAYMENT

Hypotheses: In our survey of NEP borrowers, we included several institutional variables that are hypothesized to be important determinants of loan repayment in microcredit programs: (1) transaction costs faced by borrowers, (2) homogeneity of borrower groups, and (3) threats of sanctions by the community or the program in the event of loan default.

Transaction costs: Transaction costs in credit delivery can be conceptualized as nonfinancial costs incurred by borrowers during pre–loan disbursement, loan disbursement and post–loan disbursement activities (Bhatt and Tang, 1998a&b). These may include costs associated with screening potential group members, group formation, agreeing on formal or informal group rules, negotiating with the lender, filling out the necessary paperwork, attending group meetings, and appraising and monitoring each other's projects. Borrowers may be less capable and motivated to repay loans if they have to bear excessive transaction costs due to mandatory training classes or complicated loan applications and repayment procedures. Excessive transaction costs can also result from "inefficiencies in lender delivery systems, such as missed investment opportunities because of delay in loan disbursement, due to the extra time spent processing a loan because the lending institution misplaces a document" (Sterns, 1991, p. 3).

Homogeneity of borrower groups: Socioeconomic homogeneity among group members may be conducive to loan repayment (Devereux and Fishe, 1993). Group members of many successful Third World lending programs, for example, come mostly from similar socioeconomic backgrounds (Ashe, 1985; Wahid, 1994; Otero and Rhyne, 1994). Regional and kinship ties also facilitate mutual monitoring among group members and create incentives for loan repayment. Thus homogeneity of *traits* among borrowers may be conducive to loan repayment.

In some cases, high repayment is not a function of socioeconomic homogeneity but of congruency in the goals of group members. For example, a group of economically deprived individuals may all work to improve their situation by engaging in a cooperative venture. Although the commonality of "being low-income" appears to be key to their collective action, in reality, it may have been the common desire to overcome poverty and to access future loans that makes these individuals overcome various obstacles to cooperation. Thus, homogeneity of *preferences* may help the group achieve high repayment rates.

Sanctions: As demonstrated theoretically by Besley and Coate (1995), social sanctions in group-based lending can in many instances lead to increased repayment rates. Field studies in Burkina Faso further indicate that repayment rates are high because the threat of *ex post* peer pressure is carried to extremes, and has even resulted in the forced sales of household items in order to recover the loan amount (World Bank, 1997). In several programs in Bangladesh, default has resulted in public embarrassment, exclusion from social events, and even community ostracism (Khandker, 1996).

The threat of sanctions by program management can also serve to enhance loan repayment. Often called "probation instruments," sanctions may include a loss of access to future services, such as credit or savings facilities (Stiglitz and Weiss, 1983; International Labour Organization, 1997).[8] They may also include the threat of penalties for late repayment and in the case of the United States, derogatory reporting to credit bureaus.

In summary, four hypotheses can be specified as follows:

H7:   An increase in borrower transaction costs decreases the chances of loan repayment.

H8 (a): An increase in trait homogeneity increases the chances of loan repayment.

H8 (b): An increase in preference homogeneity increases the chances of loan repayment.

H9:   Borrowers who expect to be sanctioned in the event of default are more likely to repay the loan.

A statistical test: The subjects for this test were the surveyed borrowers of the NEP program. These borrowers had participated in the lending program between 1989 and 1996 and had received group loans. Specifically, the 52 borrowers who were initially selected for the study were part of 11 credit groups. A total of 26 completed surveys were collected. In addition, several rounds of interviews with selected borrowers and program officials were conducted.

Table 4.4 shows the distribution of repayment performance of the entire population as well as the survey respondents, and

Table 4.4. Repayment performance for NEP in California

Category	Number of Borrowers (Sample)	%	Number of Borrowers (Population)	%
Repayments	11	42	22	40
Losses	15	58	30	60
Total	26	50	52	100

Table 4.5. Definition of independent variables for NEP in California

Variable	Description
T_EASE	Perceived ease and convenience before and after loan disbursement services
HOMTRAIT	Perceived homogeneity of the traits of group members
HOMPREF	Perceived homogeneity of the preferences of group members
SANCTION	Presence or absence of a perceived threat of sanctions imposed by either community members, program management, or both, in the event of loan default

Table 4.6. Logit model of repayment performance for NEP in California

Outcome variable REPAY=1, N=26

Variable	Coefficient	Wald Chi-Square	Probability Value
INTERCEPT	−13.77	2.79	0.095
T_EASE	2.51	3.06	0.080[a]
HOMTRAIT	1.96	1.77	0.183
HOMPREF	−0.84	0.52	0.472
SANCTION	2.95	4.85	0.028[b]
pseudo R^2	0.4034		

[a] Significant at 0.1 level
[b] Significant at 0.05 level

table 4.5 provides definitions of the independent variables. A logit model is specified that consists of two probabilities associated with the dependent variable REPAY, which takes on a value of 1 for loan repayment and 0 for loan default. Table 4.6 provides the results of the regression. Among the independent variables, T_EASE and SANCTION are statistically significant at the 0.10 and 0.05 levels respectively. The two variables HOMTRAIT and HOMPREF are not statistically significant.

Discussion: The statistical results suggest that when borrowers incur fewer transaction costs, they tend to have higher repayment rates. Further, the probability of loan repayment increases when the perceived threats of sanctions in the event of loan default increase. Finally, loan repayment is related to neither trait-homogeneity nor preference-homogeneity of the borrower's group.

The fact that decreasing lender-imposed transaction costs enhances loan repayment is consistent with the literature on microcredit program design. Otero and Rhyne (1994), for example, emphasize that disadvantaged entrepreneurs value convenience, ease, and flexibility of credit access more than low interest rates and fees. Many programs in the United States, however, do not focus on minimizing borrower transaction costs (Bhatt et al., 1999b). For a person who needs a microloan for working capital purposes, waiting 45 to 90 days to secure a $1,000 loan can result in lost business opportunities and in some cases, in the demise of the business itself. It is therefore important that lenders do away with bureaucratic processes that often result in lengthy loan applications and inordinate waiting periods for loan approval.

Some observers might argue that waiting periods are needed for providing borrowers with training and technical assistance so that credit is disbursed only to those who have the capacity to use the credit prudently. While the logic of building the capacity of entrepreneurs is sound, the provision of these services marks a significant departure from the practice of most of the successful Third World microcredit programs, such as Latin America's ACCION International, which offer little training or technical assistance to their borrowers.

In fact, this is precisely where microcredit programs in the United States differ fundamentally from many of those in the Third World. Most successful microcredit programs in developing countries prefer to make loans to the *working and entrepreneurial* poor; that is, those who have been engaged in a business for a couple of years when they apply for a loan. Such entrepreneurs often need the capital to grow an *ongoing* income-generating venture. They usually know exactly how the loan will be used[9] and what kinds of returns to expect from their investment. Given that a market already exists for the goods or services produced by these entrepreneurs, the chance of a loan default occurring because of a nonviable business idea is relatively low.

For most microcredit programs in the United States, such as those studied here, loans are made to a mix of existing and start-up entrepreneurs. In the case of NEP, our interviews with borrowers revealed that peer borrowers were engaged in unprofitable ventures. In some cases, they had no significant sales and found it very difficult to sustain the business over the long term. In other cases, borrowers had no prior experience in running a business at all.

To ensure that borrowers had appropriate management and business capacity, program managers in NEP required *all* participants to undergo general business training. While this kind of business training provided useful information, it did not provide start-up participants with the ability to assess the market potential of their ideas. Further, it proved to be costly for existing entrepreneurs who needed loans—in some cases immediately— to capitalize on business opportunities. Participants in the focus group sessions also indicated that the "guest speakers" such as the attorneys, accountants, and small-business consultants who led the sessions, often used technical jargon that the participants seldom understood. As a result, the classes were ultimately vehicles for "one-way" information flow from experts to the training participants. The content of the classes was generic and left the participants wondering how they could use the training to assess the market feasibility of their business ideas. Not surprisingly, most start-up businesses failed over time. Program officers felt that in many cases it was the inability to cope with personal or household emergencies that ultimately led to business failure. In any event, our survey revealed that only 5 of the 26 borrowers were still operating their businesses. Interviews with three of these five entrepreneurs suggested that two of them were struggling to make ends meet.

In addition to the transaction costs created by such training sessions, lax management practices and inefficient loan tracking also imposed high transaction costs on some borrowers. Interviews indicated that frequent changes in program staff at NEP led to misplaced loan documents and loss of time as prospective borrowers called repeatedly to inquire about their loan approval status. The NEP executive director acknowledged that she could not get loan officers to stay for more than six months. A key reason was the program's inability to offer competitive salaries and benefits to individuals who were adept at loan packaging and credit analysis.

The finding that perceived threats of sanctions increase loan repayment is also consistent with an argument in the microcredit literature that *ex ante* peer support might not be the reason for the high repayment rates of overseas group-based programs. It is rather the threat of sanctions that alleviates the moral hazard problem created by the absence of traditional collateral. In the context of Third World lending programs, the costs of defaulting include not only the loss of future credit but also public embarrassment and the loss of social standing. The fear of such embarrassment, however, was not present among NEP borrowers, because no one ever paid off anyone else's loan. Those who had defaulted on the loan claimed that their action never caused any other group members to be liable for their debts.

Interviews with selected participants confirmed that few feelings of reciprocity and trust existed among group borrowers, especially when it came time to help group members make payments that they were unable to make. Although the borrowers felt very positively about NEP's focus on group-based learning and support, there seemed to be an unwillingness to share personal financial information with one's peers, much less be liable for their debts. The joint liability principle, in the case of this program, existed only on paper. Program staff confirmed that it was neither followed nor enforced.

When borrowers were asked the question "What did you think would happen if you did not repay the loan?", 65 percent replied that they personally would not have felt good about having defaulted. Twenty-three percent stated that they feared losing access to future services. *None* of the respondents mentioned public embarrassment as a cost of default, while only 12 percent said they feared that NEP would initiate legal action.

An analysis of NEP's records suggests why most borrowers did not fear being sanctioned by the program. In some cases, default was never even noticed because of a lack of adequate record keeping. In one instance, the same individual was approved for four loans between 1991 and 1996 totaling more than $30,000 (including two individual loans), even though this borrower had paid off only her first $500 loan. While such cases might have been the result of administrative failures, they sent a wrong signal to other existing and prospective borrowers who felt that default would not be sanctioned but rather forgotten. In other words, the costs of defaulting were perceived to be quite low.

Finally, although the finding that neither trait nor preference homogeneity was related to loan repayment runs counter to conventional wisdom on the subject (see, for example, Huppi and Feder, 1990), it seems to be consistent with the results of two empirical investigations. The first is Hulme and Mosely's (1996) study of repayment performance of borrowers at the BancoSol program in Bolivia. They found that the economic homogeneity of group members did not correlate positively with loan repayment rates. The second is Zeller's (1998) study of credit groups in Madagascar, in which he concluded that "policy makers and program managers should be aware that the often-postulated homogeneity among group members has trade-offs by reducing the group's ability to repay loans" (p. 618).

Why might homogeneity not be an important determinant of loan repayment? One explanation may be that members of homogeneous groups share covariant risk. In other words, when group members belong to similar businesses, they are all likely to be impacted, usually at about the same time, by factors that negatively affect their ability to generate revenues or profits.[10] But the success of ACCION San Antonio in recovering loans made to groups of taxi drivers raises doubts about the explanatory power of this theory.

Another possible explanation is that homogeneous groups of very poor people who borrow to start businesses are less likely to own financial assets that can allow them to repay the debts of peers who experience personal or business problems. It is because of this likelihood (as well as the low levels of profitability of businesses launched by very poor borrowers in the United States) that some lenders such as ACCION and Working Capital prefer to lend not to the poorest individuals who want to start businesses but to low- and moderate-income entrepreneurs with relatively higher levels of asset holdings and experience in self-employment.

A third explanation might lie in an argument by Eiinor Ostrom (1997) that more important than the degree of homogeneity of the group seeking to achieve collective action is the extent to which group members share similar norms about trust and reciprocity. In other words, the success of group-based, joint-liability programs is likely to be greater when communities possess high reserves of social capital, since mutually shared views and agreements are fundamental to creating stable expectations and credible commitments among members in a group. It is precisely such social capital that seems to be lacking in America's inner cities (Putnam, 1993b), in which, ironically, all the four programs being studied were located.

The above views raise the question of whether group-based lending is indeed an effective risk-reducing technique for delivering credit to the poorest in America's inner cities. Some might answer in the affirmative, arguing that social capital can be created and that it is the potential of microcredit to achieve the dual objectives of economic *and* social development that makes it a unique intervention. But others such as Putnam (1993a) might suggest otherwise, lamenting that social capital has deep historical roots. Where "civicness" is present, it tends to persist; where it is not, it cannot be created easily. Indeed, as shown by recent advances in evolutionary game theory (and as is often the case in everyday life!), it is quite possible to have infinitely repeated games that favor equilibrium featuring perpetual defection (Sethi and Somanathan, 1996).

IMPLICATIONS

This chapter analyzes the determinants of loan repayment for four microcredit programs in the United States. Records of these programs show that higher levels of education and greater proximity to the lending agency increase a borrower's chance of loan repayment, while the borrower's gender does not appear to affect chances of repayment. Furthermore, our survey and interviews of borrowers of one particular program, NEP, indicate several institutional factors that are conducive to higher chances of loan repayment. These include low transaction costs for accessing loans and high borrower costs in the event of default.

The experiences of NEP are typical of unsuccessful programs across the United States and provide valuable lessons for program designers. In this case we found that members of some borrower groups even lived in different cities. Lax program management and lack of oversight led staff to form groups themselves to "get done" with the group formation process. The groups were provided general business training, and those who attended all the training sessions were awarded certificates of completion. In principle, graduation was also contingent upon the development of business plans. In practice, few efforts were made to assess the feasibility of the proposed plans, and "graduates" of the group-training program were automatically eligible for loans. Although the borrowers enjoyed the interaction and exchange of ideas with their group members, there was little group support or peer pressure when it came time to make good on a nonrepayment by a fellow group member. No one wanted to be held responsible for anyone else's debt. The group-liability principle existed on paper only—it was never enforced.

Access to future credit was never cut off for groups whose members did not repay for their defaulting peers. As such, individuals did not fear being sanctioned socially, by their own group members or other community members, in the event of default. Further, since the agency itself never took the problem of loan defaults seriously, defaulters did not fear being sanctioned by the program staff. No legal action was taken on defaulters, nor was any effort made to provide them with appropriate technical assistance once they stopped making payments. And finally, in a number of cases, due to lack of appropriate record keeping, default was not noticed at all. It was probably a combination of all the above factors that rendered this federal microcredit demonstration project nonviable after eight years of operation.

Although the results of this study cannot be generalized, when they are considered in conjunction with other available empirical and theoretical evidence (Bhatt et al., 1999a&b; Schreiner, 1998, 1999c&d; Servon, 1999), certain implications can be drawn to inform microcredit program design in the United States.

Specifically, those who are interested in microcredit initiatives as a way of achieving both economic and social development need to be aware that they are shouldering great risks and costs as they try to replicate Third World service delivery models in the United States. Unlike lenders in developing countries who make up for the lack of tangible collateral with such collateral substitutes as social capital, lenders in the United States, especially those operating in the inner city, seldom have access to such reliable substitutes.[11] When unsecured loans are made based on "imaginary" collateral substitutes such as community connectedness, trust, and reciprocity that seem to exist quite minimally, especially with respect to cross-guaranteeing loans,[12] there are probably only two possible costs confronting a loan defaulter. One is the lender's "termination threat," which results in loss of future loans. The second is *personal* (not public) embarrassment, which often depends on how one feels about not repaying debt.

Regarding the first: the threat of losing access to future loans is an effective sanctioning mechanism only when borrowers are highly dependent on future credit. When loans are made to those who are not engaged in income-generating activities on the one hand, or to those who have access to other means of income on the other, such dependency tends to be quite low. NEP made most of its loans to such "low loan dependency" borrowers; as a result, the threat of "termination" was insufficient to induce conformance to agreed-upon group and program rules. In regard to the second: one-on-one interviews with borrowers, as well as NEP staff and board members, suggested that although perceptions of personal embarrassment upon default varied from person to person, on balance, the number of people who did not care about such embarrassment probably exceeded those who did. When programs make unsecured loans to individuals who have few incentives to maintain long-term relationships with the program and who do not have to face any major costs upon defaulting, goals of achieving high loan-repayment rates, such as those obtained in some successful Third World programs, are at best quixotic propositions.

Thus, to be viable in the long run, microcredit programs in the United States need to take systematic efforts to maximize incentives for repayment. The results of this investigation highlight some possible strategies. First, compared with their counterparts in the Third World, microentrepreneurs in the United States are faced with a more competitive market environment and with more difficulties in developing profitable businesses. To enhance repayment, it is important for microcredit programs to identify potential borrowers who actually have the capacity to operate profitable businesses.[13]

It is, therefore, important for microcredit policy makers and program designers to conduct a strategic assessment of an area's economic base. For example, microenterprises are more likely to be viable when they offer goods and services within high-growth industry clusters and in areas where there exists an unmet consumer demand and high income-densities. Business sustainability and growth provide borrowers with incentives to maintain an ongoing relationship with the lender. A region's economic analysis might reveal that, in addition to capital, microentrepreneurs need assistance in developing industry-specific technical skills on the one hand and business management and problem solving skills on the other hand. Our empirical analysis suggests, for example, that one's educational level has a positive impact on loan repayment. It appears that human capital of microentrepreneurs may be an important determinant of success in the United States.

Second, if knowledge of business is important, does it mean that microcredit programs ought to provide or even mandate extensive training for borrowers? We caution against such a recommendation, because as shown in our empirical analysis, high transaction costs imposed on borrowers tend to decrease repayment. This is indeed the problem with some programs that require various forms of procedures and training before making funding available to borrowers. Since it is inherently difficult to develop a training curriculum that is useful for a wide variety of business operations, many general-purpose training requirements often turn out to create unnecessary burdens on borrowers, without actually improving their chances of success in business.

While business training may build self-esteem and social capital, its "completion" should not be equated with business viability. The focus of training and technical assistance needs to change from "completion" and "graduation" to assessing the feasibility of proposed plans for business start-up or expansion. Does the idea make sense in business terms? Has the entrepreneur mistaken the creation of a product/service with the existence of a market for it? For start-up entrepreneurs, can the market support the business's projected sales? How long will it take for the business to break even? Does the loan applicant have the necessary resources, from both the business and from other sources, to support living expenses until that time? In many instances, answering these fundamental questions does not require lengthy curricula and elaborate instruction schedules. In fact, programs can often assist a microentrepreneur assess the viability of a proposed business by engaging her in a couple of hours of "problem solving" technical assistance.

Third, the banking system in the United States has often been criticized for undermining the poor by failing to provide adequate banking facilities close to where they live (Dymski, 1996). If microcredit programs are supposed to be a means of supplementing the inadequacies of the formal banking system, it is important that these programs are located close to their clients. Being close to the clients is not just a convenience to them but also a way to promote financial discipline on the part of the borrowers. As borrowers have more incentives to maintain a long-term relationship with a funding source that is perceived to be "stable" as well as convenient for them, they have greater incentives to repay loans for the sake of maintaining that relationship. Such an argument is supported by our empirical analysis, which shows that proximity is conducive to repayment.

Last but not least, programs need to adopt effective sanctioning mechanisms against loan default. While social pressure from co-borrowers can have sanctioning effects on those who default, such mechanisms don't work as well in communities with lower social capital. In such circumstances, programs need to ensure that lending decisions are based on a sound assessment of a borrower's debt capacity. In addition, programs must develop strong accounting and management systems so that they can keep track of repayment records and take action, legal as well as programmatic, against late payments and nonrepayment. To develop and maintain such a system requires both resource and policy commitments from funders and program managers. Yet such commitments are crucial for the long-term viability of microcredit programs.

NOTES

1. Other terms often used interchangeably to describe delinquency are *past due, arrears,* and *overdue*. All of them imply that the loan has an amount that is owed and has not been paid.

2. This can include staff time spent in calling and visiting borrowers, initiating legal proceedings, or liquidating collateral.

3. A loan loss reserve is an account that represents the amount of outstanding principal that a program does not expect to recover. In other words, it is a current estimate of future repayment performance. The value of the account is usually based on historical data regarding loan defaults and an aging schedule of loans past due. The account is recorded as a negative asset on the balance sheet and is adjusted to reflect portfolio risk. The rationale and appropriate technique for creating loan loss reserves are provided in Christen (1997).

4. We were, however, faced with several constraints in the data collection and analysis process. Not all four agencies maintained good records; in fact, in the case of WDA and NEP, we were told that records for some borrowers had either not been kept or had been misplaced. While NEP provided us with direct access to client files, the other three agencies denied such access, claiming that the information was proprietary in nature. The three agencies made available to us pertinent and selected information from client files. As a result, only a limited number of socioeconomic characteristics of the borrowers could be analyzed for this study, determined mostly by whether the information about a particular characteristic could be obtained for all four programs.

5. Such arguments are often based on the views of such scholars as Goldsmith and Blakely (1992), who have made a strong case in discussing the feminization of poverty in America.

6. In addition to these variables, several other control variables are included in the logit equation. Specifically, four dummy variables are included to represent the four programs being studied. The programs are labeled P1, P2, P3, and P4, and are in no particular order (officers of two of the programs did not want their agencies compared to the other study institutions). One of the four dummy variables is dropped in the actual

estimation of the equation, and in this case, it is the dummy variable for the program P4. In addition to the dummy variables, interaction variables with intercorrelations less than 0.75 are also included as controls.

7. Although lenders in developing countries often explain the logic of mobile banking in terms of lowering a borrower's transaction costs, in reality, that is only part of the picture. A key motivation for doing so is to engage in "intensive loan collection" by increasing the pressure to repay (Hulme and Mosely, 1996, p. 24).

8. Stiglitz and Weiss (1983) refer to these as "termination threats" by the lender. Their model shows that lenders refuse to make future loans to defaulters (instead of simply raising the interest rates charged on future loan periods) primarily because such a mechanism is useful in preventing group borrowers from colluding and deciding not to pay.

9. This might even include nonbusiness uses of funds.

10. The chances of loan losses due to covariant group risk are especially high in Third World agrarian communities where project productivity and profits depend to a great extent on natural factors such as rainfall levels. Given this challenge, lenders and borrowers adopt many techniques to reduce exposure to covariant risk: use of fields adjacent to rivers during the dry season, cultivation of different soil types in land-abundant areas, off-farm income diversification, grouping farmers who cultivate crop (for example, rice) in irrigated lowlands with households that specialize in rain-fed upland, and so on (Zeller, 1998).

11. This seems to be consistent with Besley's (1995) observation that those who theoretically design group-based credit arrangements and subsequently formulate policies and programs often create institutions that are inefficient. This is usually because "often notoriously absent from such models are ideas . . . such as the social capital embodying the cumulative experience of the relevant population" (p. 124).

12. Several immigrant communities in the United States have their own rotating savings and credit associations that are quite successful in financing business start-ups. Examples include the Cambodian *Toene Tin*, the Korean *Kye*, and the Salvadorian *Cundina*. Entrepreneurs from these and several other communities prefer to depend on their own "informal" saving-and-lending groups than to approach "formal" institutions such as

community-based microcredit programs, which often impose high transaction costs for borrowing. In addition, as is discussed in chapter 5, many immigrants do not have information about and access to microlenders and their services, since agencies do not engage in intensive outreach efforts to spread the word, win community trust, and recruit these entrepreneurs.

13. The high credit risks associated with lending to low-income individuals is probably why experienced lenders such as ACCION focus on low-moderate income entrepreneurs in the United States. These individuals demonstrate greater capacity to handle debt.

CHAPTER FIVE

Sustainability

The performance of microcredit initiatives in the United States has been less successful than was expected by advocates and policy makers. Some programs have been designed employing faulty assumptions regarding the characteristics and constraints of the targeted populations. Others have suffered from lax or technically incompetent administration. Combinations of one or more of these factors have led to high loan losses on the one hand and very high administrative costs on the other.

As a result, in spite of large public and private sector investments, many such initiatives struggle to survive. Although they may have been successful in cultivating an entrepreneurial spirit among those who cherished financial self-sufficiency, they failed to communicate the need for financial discipline among most borrowers and, by default, acted for the most part as grant-making bodies rather than lending agencies. Most such micro-credit programs did not focus on sustainability at both the program and client levels, and they may have defeated the very purposes for which they were established—promoting the development of small-scale entrepreneurship.

Nelson (1994) argues that although most microcredit practitioners do not like to address the issue of sustainability, it is indeed "the goal everyone would like to achieve" (p. 18). While a majority of the programs do not aim to become financially self-sufficient, most do want to be operationally sustainable, in the sense that they do not want to go out of business. In fact, according to Nelson (1994), for most agencies sustainability is a moral imperative:

> Inherent in [a] commitment to provide credit is the responsibility to clients to ensure the permanency of that access. The need to achieve [sustainability] . . . imposes a discipline on the organization that enhances its performance. [For example] . . . Working Capital believes that sustainability is a mindset that must inform every thread on the screw of project design. Indeed, [this is] the rationale behind every aspect of its program, from the target group to its response to client demand for training—self-taught teaching modules. . . ." (pp. 18–19)

Despite the generally accepted need for sustainability, many U.S. programs struggle to keep afloat (Bhatt et al., 1999a&b). Indeed, according to a survey conducted by the Aspen Institute (1999), 80 percent of the microenterprise programs nationwide indicate their biggest concern is "programmatic sustainability." This chapter examines typical social, financial, and administrative challenges that may explain the nonviability of such microcredit programs. First, we examine challenges related to recruiting clients and building their human capital. Next, we discuss difficulties in reducing the risks and costs of lending. Finally, we explore constraints that arise from inappropriate administrative policies and governance structure and provide some concluding comments.

THE PROBLEM OF SOCIAL INTERMEDIATION

Social intermediation refers to the process of interacting with and engaging prospective borrowers in order to recruit them and make them "loan ready." As such, social intermediation can also be viewed as an investment in building up the human capital of entrepreneurs (Bennett and Goldberg, 1993). Many microcredit programs in the United States, however, have been ineffective in increasing outreach and in helping clients build appropriate human capital.

Program outreach: Microcredit programs in the United States have experienced challenges in increasing the breadth and depth of outreach. In this regard, the breadth of outreach can be assessed by the number of people who are provided financial services, while the depth of outreach can be measured by the program's ability to reach the poorest segments of society.

Breadth: Among the 16 California microcredit programs surveyed by Bhatt et al. (1999b), the average number of loans disbursed was 7 per year, with 20 being the maximum. The average number of loans outstanding was 25 per program. If these numbers are representative of programs in the United States, and assuming that there are 400 microcredit programs active in the country, the entire microcredit industry in the country is serving around 10,000 microentrepreneurs per year. This is a tiny portion of the 15 million potential microentrepreneurs estimated to be present in the United States (Burrus and Stearn, 1997).

Limited scale is not just characteristic of new programs in the United States; many well-established programs also handle limited numbers of loans annually. According to an Aspen Institute study, the average number of loans made annually by the seven leading microcredit programs in the country was about 72 (Edgcomb et al., 1996). Even highly experienced programs such as ACCION find scaling up a major challenge (Burrus and Stearn, 1997). During 1991–1996, each ACCION associate made an average of 200 loans per year. Given that ACCION is a credit-led program and perhaps one of the most "efficiency conscious" programs in the country, such statistics suggest that younger programs seeking to increase the breath of their outreach will face serious challenges.

The inability to expand portfolios, at least in the case of programs in California, has not been caused by a lack of capital. Only 1 of the 16 programs surveyed by Bhatt et al. (1999a&b) had utilized all of its funds, and the average loan fund utilization (measured by the ratio of the average portfolio to the loan fund capitalization) was around 50 percent. In fact, one program manager reported that despite having had a loan fund in place for three years, the agency had not made a single loan. A key reason for excess capacity and idle capital was an inability to find qualified applicants who would be likely to repay the loans.

In this regard, it is important to note that many microcredit programs assess borrower risk in ways that are not very different from traditional lenders. Specifically, lacking recourse to group guarantees for ensuring high repayment rates, many microcredit programs in the United States apply stringent criteria for screening borrowers. For instance, in their survey of 16 microcredit programs in California, Bhatt et al. (1999a&b) found that the top three reasons programs rejected applications were problems with credit history, poorly prepared applications, and inadequate cash flow. Ironically, these reasons quite closely resemble those cited by Dymski and Veitch (1991) as the top three reasons banks deny small-business loans: debt/income too high, inadequate capital or collateral, and poor credit histories. Unable to assess risks in nontraditional ways (some alternative strategies for analyzing risk associated with microloan prospects are considered in chapter 6), programs often run credit reports on individual loan applicants and require borrowers to find a salaried co-signer and collateral for their loans, especially if the loans are greater than $2,500. Since many individuals in low-income communities suffer from poor credit and lack of assets, it is possible that many microentrepreneurs may not be approaching lenders at all because of a fear of rejection. Further, programs may find themselves unable to expand portfolios because they do not employ nontraditional techniques for evaluating the credit risks associated with many such prospective borrowers.

Another difficulty in scaling up relates to marketing and outreach techniques. In the Third World, program officers spend months in villages, getting to know the microentrepreneurs and their families by conducting door-to-door outreach campaigns. Our interviews with the staff of the four microcredit programs studied revealed that they invested little time in personal outreach and depended more on flyers, public service announcements, and newspaper advertisements to "get the word out" about their loan programs. For many managers, the key reason for not engaging in intense outreach was the lack of resources to hire and retain qualified staff.

While underwriting criteria and service delivery techniques may hinder outreach, legal considerations also make client recruitment challenging. Informal sector activities such as street vending are still illegal in many parts of the country. Marketing and outreach activities become challenging when there is a relatively low density of easily identifiable and "visible" microentrepreneurs.

Depth: Microcredit programs have also encountered many difficulties in recruiting their original target market—people in the poorest segments of society. Although most microcredit programs in the United States have a mission to serve the low-income population, many of them also have substantial numbers of clients who live above the poverty line. For instance, Aspen Institute's study of seven of the oldest and most representative microcredit programs reveals that 62 percent of program participants were not low-income (Edgcomb et al., 1996).[1] ACCION, an international pioneer in microlending, reports that about 87 percent of its clientele is nonpoor (Himes and Servon, 1998). Seventy-two percent of the clients of another major microcredit program, Working Capital, are reported to have incomes above the poverty line (Anthony and Smith, 1996).

The fact that most U.S. programs are serving a majority of "nonpoor" clients may not be a bad thing; it can be explained by the fact that microentrepreneurs who have been successful in starting a business and increasing their personal incomes may no longer be classified as poor. These business owners are likely to be better suited for the competitive U.S. market. Often, lack of capital might be the key reason that such individuals are unable to grow their businesses. On the other hand, the lack of debt capacity among low-income entrepreneurs may be another reason that programs such as ACCION do not target low-income individuals. This is especially true for programs that make operational sustainability a priority.

Finally, serving the poor may not be consistent with the mission of many microcredit programs. For example, according to Aspen Institute's survey of 341 microenterprise programs in the United States, 44 percent of the programs ranked "job creation/business development" as their first priority, and only 29 percent listed "poverty alleviation/individual income increase" as their top priority (Aspen Institute, 1999). Given the high priority accorded by many programs to "job creation/business development," it is not surprising that they end up serving individuals who tend to come from the more educated and non-poor segments of the population.

Building human capital: In addition to problems with client outreach, some programs have failed to help their clients build appropriate human capital.

For example, Ehlers and Main (1998) conducted a three-year ethnographic study of MicroFem, a private nonprofit microenterprise development agency in the western United States. Out of the 96 women who responded to their survey, which was mailed to 1,837 trainees, 34 had started businesses between 1989 and 1994. Only 7 of the 13 respondents reporting profits said they made more than $500 a month. The authors' field experience suggests why so many businesses may have been nonviable:

> A significant amount of the "Begin-a-Biz" curriculum taught at MicroFem reinforced and perpetuated many of the romanticized visions associated with microenterprise without honestly confronting . . . the problems women face in the business world. . . . Although class instructors appeared to be taking clients seriously, we found that the training did little to empower women to make sound choices about their productive roles. . . . Encouraged by the instructors to feel good about being in business, clients were actually being trained to insert themselves into a disadvantaged sector of the business world without the opportunity or the tools to achieve the economic independence that MicroFem promised. . . . (p. 436)

The content of the training classes was of special concern to the researchers:

> Instructors lectured for hours on marketing strategies or cash flow projections, giving these business beginners too

much new material and no chance to participate, discuss, or apply what they were learning. . . . In summary, we discovered that much of the training that MicroFem pursued with its clients sidestepped the reality that they would face as women business owners. Never were they instructed to critically evaluate whether microenterprise was a feasible option for them, . . . [n]or was the microenterprise itself critically analyzed, and real difficulties, obstacles, and barriers that clients would encounter in business start-up and management were not exposed. (pp. 434–435)

Our study of the NEP training program revealed similar issues. NEP required mandatory entrepreneurial training for loan applicants. Such programs, however, focused more on making the participants "feel good" about their business ideas and less on assessing the viability of their business plans. The training failed to equip "graduates" with the knowledge and skills needed to assess the market potential of their venture start-up or growth ideas. In some instances, the training provided was so generic that it was hardly of any use to participants, who ultimately needed to evaluate if their *specific* ventures had a good chance of being profitable in the marketplace. It is, for example, not very useful to force prospective borrowers who have hobbies instead of businesses to undergo mandatory training on financial statement analysis or to listen to "guest speakers" such as attorneys and investment bankers talk about their life experiences. In fact, engaging participants in such activities probably does more harm than good, since it diverts them from assessing the feasibility of their ventures to attending training sessions and completing nonviable business plans simply to earn a "completion" certificate and qualify for loans.

The NEP program staff, for example, often asked training graduates what they could do if they were provided with $500. Loans were extended to most individuals who responded by coming up with almost any "use" of funds—from buying software for their computers to printing flyers for marketing purposes. Often, individuals in the start-up phases of their business did not know exactly what they needed the money for. Instead, they "made up" loan requests and proposals simply to acquire the capital being offered by the agency. Even though they "completed" business plans, most borrowers did not have viable business ideas. Low levels of revenues coupled with the lack of other sources of income made it difficult for them to service their debt. As a result, NEP's loan losses after eight years of microlending were at 60 percent.

When loans are disbursed to microentrepreneurs without an appropriate assessment of their debt capacity, the likelihood of loan losses is considerable (von Pischke, 1991).

THE PROBLEM OF FINANCIAL INTERMEDIATION

Financial intermediation refers to a lender's ability to create value through managing risks and minimizing transaction costs (von Pischke, 1991). Many microcredit programs in the United States have failed on one or both of these criteria.

Inability to manage risk: Microcredit has gained popularity in the United States because it seemingly allows people to borrow money despite the fact that they lack tangible collateral. Indeed, examples from the developing world where such unsecured lending has succeeded are often cited in policy circles in the United States, and program designers have been quick to recommend the philosophy of uncollateralized lending. Yet policy makers and practitioners have often paid little attention to the fact that in successful Third World programs, tangible collateral is replaced by collateral substitutes. These substitutes include (1) interlinked contracts; (2) personal knowledge of the borrower's household income and the extent to which it can be accessed to service the debt; (3) a borrower's entrepreneurial history and personal reputation; and (4) a borrower's membership in informal savings groups (Hulme and Mosely, 1996).

Furthermore, successful programs make loans based on accurate assessments of microentrepreneurs' debt capacity. This means that the combination of cash generated from clients' businesses and household incomes is both adequate and available to make timely loan repayments. The need to evaluate debt capacity has also been underscored by von Pischke (1991):

> Lenders are able to recover loans on schedule only when the repayment capacity of the borrower equals or exceeds debt service, which consists of principal and interest due for payment. Borrowers are able to repay their loans on time without suffering hardship only when their repayment capacity equals or exceeds the debt service due according to the loan contract. These simple, self-evident relationships define the role that credit plays in development and influence the fate of efforts to expand the frontier of formal finance. (p. 277)

Finally, many group-based microcredit programs in the United States have failed to recognize that Third World initiatives rely heavily on the high reserves of social capital—defined as shared norms, personal trust, and reciprocity (Putnam, 1993)—that is characteristic of physically proximate and socially "connected" communities in many developing countries. Such social capital often makes the mutual liability mechanism a reliable collateral substitute. Yet according to Taub (1998),

> [The] group process is unlikely to be a useful tool for generating repayment . . . in the United States unless the group

had a long term prior basis for being in existence so that members had meaningful social ties with each other. Individuals who are strangers and who have no real stake in each other's success (or failure) are ineffective as a peer pressure group, though they may provide support and other types of assistance for each other. (p. 68)

Indeed, most low-income communities within the United States, especially those in the inner city, lack the social capital that results from repeated interactions, reciprocity, and shared norms of conduct (Putnam, 1993b). In such areas, the joint-liability principle is difficult even to communicate to borrowers, much less to put in practice. In places where group lending is implemented in this manner, without the presence of any collateral or reliable collateral substitutes, the chances of reducing default through group-based lending are likely to be low.

The performance of both the NEP and WDA programs supports the above argument. Although group guarantees officially served as a collateral substitute in the NEP program, none of the borrowers was willing to support fellow group members when they missed loan payments. Similarly, in the case of WDA, the mutual liability principle lacked credibility as a collateral substitute because of the lack of social capital among the inner-city borrowers. This, in addition to the fact that most borrowers' businesses turned out to be nonviable, was a key reason why the agency's portfolio suffered from high risks[2] (averaging 23 percent for 1994, see table 5.1) and default rates (averaging 18 percent, see table 5.2)—performance indicators that are quite inferior to those experienced by effective Third World microcredit programs (the most successful of which have defaults ranging from 3 to 5 percent).

Inability to minimize costs: Microcredit programs are much more costly to operate in the United States than similar pro-

Table 5.1. Portfolio at risk for California-based WDA program

	June 1993	December 1993	June 1994	December 1994	Average
Percent	24	17	23	26	23

Source: Agency

Table 5.2. Annual loan loss for California-based WDA program

	1992	1993	1994	Average
Percent loss	12	24	17	18

Source: Agency

grams overseas. Not only are the costs associated with making and servicing a small loan high compared to the income earned from interest and fees charged on the loan, other nonfinancial costs such as those associated with borrower outreach are also very high.

To reduce administrative costs, programs often rely less on formal screening, monitoring, and enforcement processes, and instead trust that either individual borrowers or groups will perform those functions effectively. Yet the latter is possible only when participants are able to internalize the costs associated with such activities or when the benefits of such involvement exceed the costs. But the lack of motivation among many inner-city borrowers to shoulder these additional responsibilities often results in the replacement of informal screening, monitoring, and enforcement mechanisms with formal ones that are costly to administer.

Cost inefficiencies were central to the demise of the WDA program. The program's financial records revealed that for the 1992–1994 period (during which the program conducted over 75 percent of its lending), the average cost per loan was $10,863, while the average loan size was $3,338. In fact, for 1994, the average cost per loan was $15,329, while the average loan size was $3,474.

THE PROBLEM OF
ADMINISTRATIVE INTERMEDIATION

Administrative intermediation refers to the practices, policies, and structures that govern the operations of a lending agency. Many U.S. microcredit programs lack effective administrative intermediation.

Since microcredit is a relatively new initiative in the United States, it lacks a clear set of industry standards, especially with regard to best practices and policies for program administration. For instance, in their analysis of 16 programs funded by the Office of Refugee Resettlement during the period 1991–1996, Else and Clay-Thompson (1998) note:

> Administrative practices were often inadequate; . . . agencies did not have well-established administrative policies and procedures. . . . For example, case records were sometimes incomplete. A few agencies had inadequate documentation of refugee status in their files at the time of the first technical assistance visit; business plans and loan applications often had inadequate personal financial information, cash flow projections for businesses, and documentation of marketing plans and financial analysis. Many programs could not produce summary data on the microenterprise participants and their businesses. (pp. 22–23)

In addition to such inadequacies, several other problems with administrative practices and policies also exist in many microcredit programs in the United States.

First, most programs do not make enhancing self-sufficiency a priority and therefore remain almost entirely dependent on outside subsidies. Funds for capitalizing microcredit programs are often obtained at concessional rates or, in some cases, acquired as grants from foundations. In the absence of any stringent market tests for returns on capital, inefficient program administrators often treat such funds as "free money" and disburse it without due diligence.[3] By failing to sanction defaulters and by sometimes making repeat loans to those who have defaulted before, program administrators send a perverse signal to existing and prospective borrowers. A culture of nonrepayment prevails and over time becomes the norm. It is only a matter of time before such subsidy-dependent programs are rendered nonviable.

Second, administrative costs of microcredit programs, especially in terms of staff salaries and basic infrastructure, are much higher in the United States when compared to many developing countries in which such programs are most successful. As a result, the administrative expenses associated with running microcredit programs in the United States are much higher, making movements toward financial sustainability challenging.

Third, most microcredit programs in the United States do not charge interest rates and fees that can cover their risks and administrative cost structures. One reason is that usury laws in the United States restrict the interest rate a lender can charge to *fully* cover costs, and perhaps make a profit. Even if a lender's first priority were self-sufficiency, it would take a lender much longer to recover costs. Another reason is that some programs believe low-income entrepreneurs should be extended subsidized credit. For instance, some programs charge interest rates as low as 2 percent, while others do not charge any fees to cover costs (see table 5.3).

Sponsors and managers who view microcredit delivery as a social policy rather than a commercial transaction are less likely to build sustainable programs.

Table 5.3. Annual interest rates and fee structures for 189 U.S. microcredit programs

	Mean	SD	Min.	Max.	Fees		
					Yes	No	Not reported
Individual lending interest rate N=146	10.53	2.44	2	18	38.4%	48.6%	13.0%
Group lending interest rate N=43	12.03	3.19	2	18	34.9%	53.5%	11.6%

Source: Data obtained from Aspen Institute and author's calculations

_Finally, problems in administrative intermediation arise because of challenges associated with program governance. Specifically, when various stakeholders—borrowers, field staff, program managers, boards of directors, and fiscal sponsors—face incompatible incentives, chances for inefficiencies are high. Program managers often find themselves unable to articulate a coherent set of goals and objectives, especially when they secure funding from multiple donors who have different criteria for assessing program success.

For instance, if sponsors insist on increasing lending volume and outreach, program officers feel the pressure to increase numbers of loans without appropriate screening. Such pressures often result in borrowers being given credit in a short time, without proper care being taken to ensure that the loans disbursed are viable. This appears to have been the case with WDA, which increased the number of loans from 17 in 1990 to 62 in 1993. Also, due to pressures from donors to increase lending volume, the agency started making more individual loans and increasing loan sizes. The agency's individual loans jumped from 2 in 1990 to 22 in 1993, while the average individual loan size increased from $2,000 to $8,325. Also, the average loan size for group loans increased from $1,667 to $2,396 in the same period, which led to an overall loan size increase from $1,735 in 1990 to $4,500 in 1993 (see table 5.4). In addition to pressures on management to increase lending volume, such increases were probably also related to the nature and mix of funds that capitalized WDA's portfolio in 1993, with some sponsors wanting to lend to start-up entrepreneurs and others wanting to lend to existing entrepreneurs.

Another conflict in stakeholder objectives was evidenced when WDA acquired loan capital from the U.S. Small Business Administration. Specifically, by acquiring SBA's Microloan Demonstration project, WDA increased its loan pool from $100,000 to $850,000 and its maximum loan amount from $5,000 to $25,000. This, however, signaled a departure from the agency's core philosophy of serving the poor. Making larger loans to individuals required officers with expertise in credit analysis and loan packaging, which the agency lacked. Larger loans that were disbursed based on trust instead of due diligence ultimately went bad. The agency thus found itself "torn" in trying to serve different types of markets and to please different sponsors—key stakeholders whose incentives were obviously misaligned.

In addition to having stakeholders with different incentives, microcredit programs such as NEP and WDA often have limited administrative resources. In such instances, monitoring loan performance becomes a challenge, and often repayment and collection schedules are not followed because the costs of such loan-tracking activities are too high for the lending agency to bear. Once loan defaults start to increase, lax procedures with respect to collections and sanctions send a negative signal to other borrowers, who see incentives in not repaying their loans. Portfolio quality thus deteriorates, and little money is left for

Table 5.4. Loan disbursement record for California-based WDA program

	1990	1991	1992	1993	1994	1995	TOTAL
GROUP LENDING							
Loans	15	47	33	40	19	0	154
Loans ($)	25,000	90,500	68,500	95,850	42,900	0	323,250
Avg. loan size ($)	1,667	1,926	2,076	2,396	2,258	0	2,099
INDIVIDUAL LENDING							
Loans	2	3	10	22	8	2	47
Loans ($)	4,000	5,000	19,300	183,148	50,895	17,500	279,843
Avg. loan size ($)	2,000	1,667	1,930	8,325	6,362	8,750	5,954
TOTAL LENDING							
Loans	17	50	43	62	27	2	201
Loans ($)	29,500	95,500	87,800	278,998	93,795	17,500	603,092
Avg. loan size ($)	1,735	1,910	2,042	4,500	3,474	8,750	3,000

Source: Agency data and author's calculations

running day-to-day operations. It is at this moment that a lending agency requests additional funds from its donors. Should such a request be granted, it just marks the beginning of another vicious circle of underperformance. This example is typical of situations faced by many program administrators in the United States, who have felt the need to submit to donor pressures and ended up implementing inappropriate programs and delivery systems.

CONCLUSION

Institutional sustainability is one of the biggest challenges facing microcredit programs in the United States. While microcredit programs that are financed in part with taxpayer funds are more likely to face the problems of inappropriate governance structures and perverse performance incentives, it is important to note that even initiatives using commercial sources of funds can be rendered unsustainable, for instance, if they are unable or unwilling to reduce transaction costs. Sustainability may also become a challenge if programs are ineffective in recruiting clients with the potential for success in entrepreneurship, in managing risks and administrative costs, and in employing technically competent managers and loan officers. In order to increase the chances of sustainability, policy makers and program designers may wish to keep in mind the various social, financial, and administrative challenges considered in this chapter.

NOTES

1. The Aspen Institute defines low-income individuals as those whose household incomes fall below 150 percent of the poverty line.

2. "Portfolio at risk" is defined as outstanding balances of loans that are more than 30 days late divided by total loans outstanding at the end of each reporting period.

3. Not all U.S. programs rely exclusively on such grants to fund their loan pools. Experienced lenders such as ACCION negotiate lines of credit or loans with banks. This capital is then "retailed" by the program in the

form of microloans. But even as ACCION enhances its financial self-sufficiency, it does need to depend on grants or donations to fund its loan loss reserve fund and its "bridge fund," which guarantees a portion of the bank funds that its affiliate programs borrow to on-lend to their clients.

CHAPTER SIX

Potential

The microcredit movement has received tremendous attention in policy circles because of its potential to improve the lives of low-income individuals by providing them with a hand up, instead of a handout, as they pursue self-employment. The movement's popularity stems from its ability to appeal to a spectrum of political ideologies: its endorsement of the free market and entrepreneurship solicits support from the Right, while its social objectives of poverty alleviation and empowerment facilitate endorsement from the Left. Indeed, it is this "win-win" promise of microfinance that makes it attractive to leaders across the world, including those in the United States (Morduch, 1999).

Although public and private sector support for microcredit initiatives has grown rapidly, most U.S. programs have come nowhere close to matching the performance and achievements of their Third World "models." We have tried to analyze why this might be so, and our framework suggests that three factors are key to the viability of microcredit programs: the constraints faced by small-scale entrepreneurs in enterprise development in general and in accessing capital in particular; the socioeconomic and institutional contexts of the communities within which lending is conducted; and the conditions under which agencies engage in social, financial, and administrative intermediation (chapter 2).

We find that although entrepreneurs perceive the lack of access to capital as being a major constraint to success in self-employment, noncapital constraints, especially the lack of revenues, also present significant challenges to microenterprise development in the United States (chapter 3). The income generated by many microentrepreneurs is insecure and risky; borrowing gets them into deeper debt than they are in to start with. Banks may decline loans to microentrepreneurs not only because of possible socioeconomic discrimination or individuals' lack of good credit and collateral but also because loan applicants' businesses have poor market potential and as a result, cannot generate the cash flows needed to service the debt. Microcredit programs serving such entrepreneurs need to pay greater attention to the entrepreneurs' ability to access markets and generate sustainable revenues to cover operating costs, repay their loans, and take a draw. An unfavorable market environment may pose a major challenge to microentrepreneurs and, by extension, to the viability of microcredit programs.

Several other factors decrease the likelihood of viability: sometimes programs do not take into account socioeconomic and institutional factors in designing products and services; in other cases, they lack sound management practices (chapter 4). Our analysis of four of the oldest microcredit "replications" in the United States suggests that factors associated with loan repayment are both similar to and different from those in successful Third World programs. On the one hand, higher loan repayment rates are associated with higher levels of education, proximity to the lending agency, lower transaction costs for accessing loans and higher borrower-costs in the event of default. On the other hand, key variables such as gender and homogeneity of borrowers do not seem to be significantly related to loan repayment. Indeed, seemingly "homogeneous" groups can actually lack social capital, rendering joint-liability arrangements meaningless. This not only increases the administrative costs associated with group maintenance, it also bolsters loan losses when borrowers are unable or unwilling to service their loans.

Loan repayment can also suffer due to poor management practices. Some programs, for instance, lack appropriate accounting and information systems for servicing loans, monitoring borrowers, and sanctioning defaulters. Borrowers who realize that a program's record keeping is lax are less motivated to repay their loans, especially when they perceive the cost of default to be low. The likelihood of default also increases when programs take a long time to disburse funds and require loan applicants to complete mandatory business training classes.

Such training requirements can impose high transaction costs, usually in the form of lost business opportunities, for many borrowers with existing businesses. Further, their "generic" formats are of little use to most start-up entrepreneurs, who need to generate business revenues that allow them to cover costs, repay their debt, and take a draw. Although business training may provide useful information and build human and social capital, its "completion" should not be equated with business viability. The focus of business development services needs to shift from "training completion" and "graduation" to assessing the market feasibility of participants' *specific* plans for business start-up and growth.

Problems of social, financial, and administrative intermediation are key barriers to program sustainability in the United States (chapter 5). Problems in social intermediation lead to the expending of inordinate amounts of time and resources on client outreach and recruitment. For example, cultural and language barriers within inner-city communities can make these activities cumbersome and expensive. Further, the inability to reach and recruit sufficient entrepreneurs engaged in income-generating activities often results in loans being extended to individuals who lack the capacity for successful self-employment. Making such prospective borrowers "loan ready" often can prove to be taxing and ineffective, especially when human-capital-building efforts such as basic training classes serve as vehicles for social empowerment rather than enterprise development. While programs that focus on individual empowerment are important for community development, policy makers need to recognize that they may not necessarily translate into the actual development of microenterprises or to the enhancement of participants' economic self-sufficiency in the short run.

Problems arise in financial intermediation due to the inability of "replicated" programs to manage risks and economize transaction costs. Many lenders, for example, engage in unsecured lending in the absence of reliable collateral substitutes. When such group- and character-based deals begin to go bad, programs implement intensive loan collection procedures and find that the administrative costs of loan monitoring and enforcement are very high. Often, it is a combination of high risks and costs that leads to the unsustainability of many programs.

Finally, a number of microcredit programs are plagued by problems of administrative intermediation that result from inappropriate development policies and governance structures. Several reasons account for these challenges. First, the availability of grants or subsidized capital and the lack of industry standards for gauging performance tend to give rise to lax administration, thereby bolstering loan losses. Second, high administrative costs of some programs significantly boost operating overhead. Third, inability under usury laws to charge interest rates and fees that can cover the cost and risk of capital—and sometimes unwillingness arising from an absence of commercial objectives—contributes to the nonviability of many programs. Finally, stakeholders such as clients, loan officers, managers, board members, and fiscal sponsors often have different goals, motivations, and priorities when they participate in such programs. The lack of incentive alignment often leads to operational inefficiencies and renders programs unsustainable.

THE MICROCREDIT POTENTIAL

Many observers have questioned the notion that microenterprise programs can effectively address the problem of poverty in the United States (Bates, 1997; Schreiner, 1999a; Servon, 1999). While many programs "target" the poorest in principle, they end up in practice serving those with above-average educations, skills, experiences in wage or self-employment, incomes, and asset holdings. This is partly because the most disadvantaged often choose not to participate in these programs. Further, as shown in the preceding chapters, even when programs recruit the poorest (including welfare recipients and chronically unemployed individuals), they face tremendous challenges in recovering loans and containing administrative costs. In fact, Schreiner (1999c) argues that such programs are unlikely to increase the number of participants who move from poverty to self-employment by more than 1 in 100 for unemployed individuals, and by more than 6 in 1,000 for those on welfare.

Similarly, based on her in-depth case studies of several credit- and training-led programs around the country, Servon (1997) argues that microenterprise "clearly is not the answer to the urban poverty problem . . . it is not geared to attract 'victims'; rather, it attracts and makes visible potential community leaders—people who are in positions to use these programs to help themselves and their businesses. . . . [M]ost participants do not fit the underclass stereotype that tends to attract the lion's share of media or federal attention" (p. 175). Indeed, such findings often raise concern as to "whether a broad-spread national proliferation of microenterprise programs, as [is often] proposed, would render sustained structural impact on poverty" (O'Regan and Conway, 1993, p. 13).

While more rigorous research is needed to accurately assess the true benefits and costs of microcredit programs in the United States, the above views seem to be consistent with the experiences of most initiatives abroad. After years of public and private investments in Third World programs, for instance, evaluations of most microcredit programs have indicated that it is generally not the poorest but the better-off low-income households who benefit from such initiatives. Indeed, for the most-disadvantaged of poor people around the world, microcredit may not be the antipoverty weapon that it is often made out to be (Hulme and Mosley, 1996; Robinson, 1996). In many circumstances, poverty alleviation objectives are likely to be more effectively furthered by other types of interventions, such as public health, education, and job and skills training. These measures may have the additional advantage, as compared to microcredit programs, of enhancing security and reducing risk in low-income communities.

Some observers may not feel comfortable with the above arguments. For example, in response to the arguments of Richard Taub (1998), and Timothy Bates and Lisa Servon (1996), who caution microenterprise programs to focus resources not on the very poor but rather on entrepreneurs with greater chances of success, Ivan Light (1998) says:

> On Taub's view, also vigorously championed by Timothy Bates and Lisa Servon, money loaned to the poor would be better utilized if loaned instead, as Taub puts it, to "real

businesses with development potential." Real businesses could hire the poor as wage earners whereas, so goes the argument, when microcredit schemes loan directly to the poor, the borrowers either lose it outright due to their incompetence or employ it ineffectively in the production of insignificant income. This is exactly the objection that Mohammad Yunus faced from bankers in Bangladesh, and its deployment . . . suggests that it is still an ideological pivot around which debate circles. Personally, I find this debate a chicken and egg stand-off since, if trickle-down economics worked, we would have no poor people in need of self-employment alternatives. (p. 3)

Light's general reference is to observers who argue that microcredit may potentially serve as an effective development tool when programs target not the poorest, but low- and moderate-income entrepreneurs who are likely to succeed and whose businesses have the capacity to productively absorb larger loans. But Servon's (1999) study of three microcredit programs— Women's Initiative for Self-Employment, Working Capital, and ACCION—suggests that fostering equity and growth may not necessarily be incompatible. According to her, for example, despite operational and philosophical differences, these programs are in fact able to "blend aspects of economic development and poverty alleviation strategies [and the] results are overwhelmingly beneficial" (pp. 73–74).

STRATEGIES FOR CAPACITY BUILDING

Although both poverty alleviation- and economic development-oriented programs face similar social, financial, and administrative challenges, with only a few exceptions (for example, Servon and Bates, 1998), not much has been written about how these challenges can be, or ever might be, addressed. For the sake of initiating debates on this matter, we next discuss several possible strategies to build program capacity by developing appropriate lending techniques, financial products, nonfinancial services, and plans for enhancing financial self-sustainability.

Lending techniques: A credit delivery system that is suited to one context may not be appropriate for another. Microcredit programs need to identify specific types of lending arrangements that are suitable for their own communities. Chami and Fischer (1995), for example, argue that community development banking in the United States is most likely to succeed where borrowers are geographically immobile, so that banks can monitor both pre- and post-lending behaviors at low costs. Bhatt and Tang (1998b) make a similar argument, suggesting that group lending strategies are more likely to succeed in communities with higher reserves of social capital and reciprocity. In communities with low social capital reserves, such as those within many inner cities in the United States (Putnam, 1993b), implementation of group lending strategies may more likely increase a program's lending risks and costs.[1]

Although many U.S. microcredit programs may not be able to rely on the "social collateral" of peer borrowers to increase program awareness or to secure their loans, they can explore alternative strategies for conducting outreach and assessing the credit risks of low-income individuals.

For increasing outreach, for example, instead of relying on such passive methods as flyers, public service announcements, and newspaper advertisements, programs may develop more proactive techniques. Since there may be a low awareness of microcredit programs among many potential borrowers, programs need to invest in intensive outreach efforts. For instance, programs can establish relationships with grassroots organizations and advocacy groups that are interested in promoting social justice. Some social entrepreneurs, for example, seek to promote social justice by running for-profit businesses that employ low-income individuals (Bhatt, 2000). Many employees of such social entrepreneurial ventures are good candidates for microentrepreneurship themselves.

In addition, microcredit programs may consider working with organizations that provide employment referral and placement services for low-income communities in specific areas. For example, LISTO, a Los Angeles–based nonprofit organization, serves as a matchmaking agency for poor Latino immigrants and private companies seeking short-term help. The agency has more than 150 members who are placed for an average of three days a week. With access to microloans, these individuals may be able to launch small businesses that allow them to work for another two or three days a week and to "patch" their earning capacities.

Another possible strategy for enhancing outreach is to use alternative methods for assessing credit risks. Such methods could include landlord references, savings records, and proofs of car payment or utility bill payments. Although it may somewhat increase program administrative costs to access such records, the strategy may help to identify low-income individuals who lack a strong credit history but have demonstrated reasonable repayment discipline in the recent past. In addition, programs might secure their loans with items such as television sets, stereo units, furniture, pieces of equipment, or cars. Although such nontraditional or "creative" collateral might not have significant market value compared to the loan amounts disbursed, they are often important to individual borrowers, and have been known to serve as effective security against willful default for some of the more prominent U.S. programs, including the Women's Self Employment Project and ACCION (Bonavoglia, 2000; Burrus, 1997).

Financial products: When financial products match market demands, lenders are likely to reduce both the risks and costs of doing business. It is therefore important that programs accurately assess financing gaps in specific geographic markets and establish market niches accordingly. Although most microcredit programs in the United States started with the strategy of offering very small loans (usually $500) to the poorest, they seldom experienced success in terms of high repayment rates and requests for repeat loans. A key reason was that a large majority of the most disadvantaged borrowers lacked the emotional, educational, and entrepreneurial capacity that is required to handle debt. As a result, these individuals could seldom put the loans to productive use. On the other hand, even the many who could be motivated and empowered through training classes found it difficult to access markets and sell their products or services on a sustainable basis.

Given this challenge, some of the more successful programs such as ACCION do not provide training but instead make available larger loans (say between $2,500 and $10,000) to a niche market—the working poor. Although this population is typically underemployed, it frequently has significant experience in the labor market and well-defined skills, often in both wage and self-employment. By engaging in part-time self-employment and putting their otherwise idle labor to productive use, some segments of this population are able to "patch" their current sources of income with their entrepreneurial earnings. Although it may not create new jobs, the "income patching" benefit of microcredit may help generate additional income that could play a key role in reducing the vulnerability of low-income individuals to sudden emergencies and income shocks that commonly haunt low-income communities. Indeed, Taub (1998) suggests that "targeting [such a] population appropriately would make [microcredit programs] more successful in generating loan volumes, making people's lives better, and moving toward self-sufficiency" (p. 68).

Another gap in the financial market is for loans between $10,000 and $50,000. Individuals who have the capacity to handle this level of debt are not necessarily low-income but typically low-moderate income. Yet they too may find it difficult to access conventional financing. Serving such entrepreneurs may well be a key opportunity for microcredit programs that seek to increase financial self-sufficiency but find it hard to generate sufficient revenues by disbursing very small loans. Another possible advantage in serving this market is that it is more likely to result in business growth and job creation (Taub, 1998).

In addition to matching financial services with market niches, microcredit programs need to tailor their loan products to the business opportunities of clients within specific niches. For example, working capital loans may be best suited for entrepreneurs in service businesses, but they may need to be complemented with equipment loans for those in the manufacturing sector. While the financing needs of some sectors may be flat throughout the year, those of others, such as entrepreneurs who sell gift baskets or Christmas trees during the holiday season, may vary seasonally. When loan sizes and terms match market demand and the entrepreneurs' cash flows, credit risks and administrative costs can be reduced substantially.

Another important, but often neglected, aspect of financial intermediation is savings mobilization. It is now well established that most banks are unwilling to bet on a microenterprise with an unproven track record. As a result, entrepreneurs generally access personal savings or informally acquired capital, not debt, to launch small-scale businesses. Given this reality, the lack of assets in low-income communities presents a significant barrier to microenterprise development.

Many low-income microentrepreneurs lack assets because they lack access and incentives to save, and in this regard, microcredit programs can play a key role. For example, they can provide individuals with information about the critical role savings can play in helping them escape the vicious cycle of no assets—no loan—no investment—no income—no assets. They can also provide potential borrowers with access to savings instruments such as Individual Development Accounts (IDA) by linking them with banks. This can be especially useful in low-income areas where bank branches are closing down due to competitive pressures (as was examined in chapter 3). Many microcredit programs that are physically close to the local communities are suited to recruit IDA prospects and link them with banks.

Most strategies for inner-city development, however, seem to focus on the credit side. Providing individuals with the access to convenient, reliable, accessible, and flexible savings facilities can help foster asset building in low-income communities. But despite the importance of savings to entrepreneurship development, it seems to be the forgotten half of urban finance policy[2] and needs urgent and immediate attention (Dymski, 1993).[3]

Nonfinancial services: Research suggests that entrepreneurs with higher levels of education are more likely to succeed (Bates, 1997). As a result, many microcredit programs require mandatory training completion as a prerequisite to accessing loans. In doing so, however, lenders incur high overhead costs (Edgcomb et al., 1996). While some organizations such as ACCION and Working Capital choose not to provide such services directly, other agencies require borrowers to undertake several hours of general entrepreneurial training, ranging from 18 hours at the Good Faith Fund to 90 hours at the Institute for Social and Economic Development (Edgcomb et al., 1996). In many cases, lending agencies are mandated by their federal sponsors to provide several sessions of training to potential borrowers. Agencies that provide such training services often end up shouldering high administrative costs, even though not all borrowers actually need such services.

What should determine if a prospective borrower needs to attend an entrepreneurial training program in order to receive a loan? Experiences from effective microcredit programs around the country suggest that when entrepreneurs are already involved in income-generating activities and are requesting working capital loans, they usually know exactly what they will use the capital for and what the sources and timing of repayment can be. Requiring such entrepreneurs to attend *mandatory* training is not advisable. In contrast, a training class may be useful for individuals who are interested in evaluating the feasibility of their business ideas (often referred to as "start-up" entrepreneurs), and perhaps for those who need to develop a plan to grow their existing ventures. Indeed, some organizations have argued that training may be "most effective when it invests in entrepreneurs who pursue GROWTH in their businesses. . . . " (Women's World Banking, 1993, p. 2; original emphasis; see also "Is Training Important?" on the following page). Similarly, Servon and Bates (1998) recommend that programs should "steer entrepreneurs away from narrow, low-income, minority markets." According to them, "Research shows that entrepreneurs who do business with a narrow, low-income population become ghettoized and limit their growth and profitability. Business stabilization and growth are more likely when the entrepreneur reaches a broader market. Microenterprise programs must help entrepreneurs to establish firms targeting emerging [market] opportunities" (p. 438). It is therefore critical for a program to assess thoroughly a client's business opportunities and likelihood of success before mandating any training.

It is also important for agencies to deliver training that is consistent with their missions. For example, while many programs' stated mission is economic development, their training sessions are often geared toward social empowerment rather than business development. While empowering individuals is certainly important for poverty alleviation and community development (Bhatt, 2000), policy makers need to recognize that it may not necessarily translate into the development of income-generating microenterprises and the reduction of lending risk.

Is Training Important?

The Women's World Banking (WWB) Experience

Over the past decade, there has been much debate among practitioners on the issue of whether training has a real impact on poor entrepreneurs. Many argue that training makes little or no difference to the performance of the client's business and that it is not cost-effective for the provider or the recipient of training to undertake it. In the view of best practice affiliates, training is important only when it is important to the client. The relevance of training can be measured by the client's willingness to contribute her time and pay a fee for the service. If training not directly related to another affiliate service is imposed as a prerequisite to accessing that service, the affiliate cannot be certain of the utility of the training to the client. She may view training merely as a hurdle to accessing credit—and not responsive to her needs. Affiliates need to assess and respond to the client needs of training in order to make a difference to clients' survival and growth in the changing market place.

It is critical that affiliates assess the impact of training on clients' income, assets, employment, and growth. Experience indicates that training can make a significant difference to microenterprise clients operating in growth sectors. Training geared to subsistence-oriented activities often costs much more than it yields in the form of clients' increased profits, incomes, or assets.

Categories for selecting target clientele may include geographic area served, business sector, income/asset level, survival versus growth oriented, individuals versus groups, start ups versus existing businesses. An affiliate may choose to avoid high risk, low growth potential sectors in the interest of meeting its impact and institutional sustainability objectives. Based on their experience, many affiliates have found that training for individuals thinking about starting a business results in a high rate of attrition with few participants actually starting businesses. For those who do, the majority of the businesses do not survive beyond the first year. Affiliates investing their resources in existing microbusinesses with growth potential may focus on training clients in non-traditional productive sectors rather than entrepreneurs selling traditional or handicraft products.

Unless affiliates focus on businesses with some potential for growth, the resulting impact of their services will be negligible. Identifying a target clientele with business growth objectives whose products have market potential is the key to developing programs that have real impact.

Source: Women's World Banking, 1993

In addition to business training, many microcredit programs in the United States are currently offering some technical assistance to clients, and policy makers are discussing the need to increase government funding for supporting such efforts. Appropriate technical assistance may be useful both before and after loan disbursement. Before loan approval, for example, a brief session with the loan applicant can help provide answers to a number of critical questions. Does the idea make sense in business terms? Has the applicant mistaken the existence of a product/service with the existence of a market for it? How long will it take for the business to break even? Does the loan applicant have the necessary resources, from both the business and other sources, to support living expenses until that time? Programs can often assess the viability of an individual's proposed business start-up or expansion plan by engaging in a couple of hours of "problem solving" technical assistance.

At the post–loan disbursement stage, technical assistance consultants may conduct regular site visits to discuss, among other things, issues about loan repayments and any current or possible future business problems. Such interactions serve two purposes. First, they send a signal to the borrower that timely loan repayment is important to the lending agency and must be given priority. This helps "document" financial discipline that is crucial to building a good credit history. Second, information gathered during such visits helps lenders detect business problems early and allows them to make available any necessary technical assistance in a timely fashion.

While providing entrepreneurs with training and technical assistance can be useful in building their human capital, programs need to ensure that these services are demand driven. Further, it is not necessary for microlenders, especially those who want to increase their financial self-sufficiency, to be involved in the *direct* provision of such services. Schreiner (1998), for instance, cites the experiences of microenterprise programs (MEPs) abroad to caution against mixing classes and loans in the same program:

> The record abroad suggests that loans and classes do not mix. . . . MEPs abroad that mixed loans and classes found that good teachers were not always good lenders and vice versa. To excuse default, the MEP claimed that borrowers

confused the gift of classes with the loan of cash. MEPs were also loath to dun defaulters whose ventures failed in spite of the use of what was taught in the classes. Perhaps the most important lesson from abroad is that MEPs should erect a firewall between the accounts of loans and of classes, if not cleave the MEP in two pieces, one that lends and one that teaches. (p. 29)

Given the large numbers of universities, community colleges, and SBA-sponsored Small Business Development Centers (SBDCs) and Women's Business Centers (WBCs) across the country that specialize in the provision of entrepreneurial training and technical assistance, microcredit programs would do well to establish collaborative partnerships with such entities. Since lending and training are specialized functions, such linkages can potentially enhance outcomes for both lenders as well as business development agencies by allowing them to do what they are best suited for.[4]

Finally, even as microcredit programs around the country increase their focus on providing nonfinancial services, policy makers should not lose sight of the fact that lack of financial resources will likely continue to be a constraint for many low- and moderate-income entrepreneurs. Many such individuals are likely to need *both* financial and nonfinancial supports, possibly at different times, in order for their enterprise development efforts to succeed. Thus the current focus on expanding training programs should not come at the expense of new strategies for deepening and widening the availability of finance in low-income communities.

Enhancing financial sustainability: Microcredit programs in the United States are faced with high overhead costs. These costs, together with the inability and unwillingness of many program operators to charge higher interest rates and loan fees, have made it difficult for the vast majority of programs to enhance financial self-sufficiency. One may argue that microcredit programs deserve subsidies, because they contribute to economic development of disadvantaged communities and provide human capital–building services whose benefits they cannot fully capture. While both arguments have merit, it is nonetheless possible for programs to move toward a higher degree of self-sufficiency without necessarily sacrificing their mission to assist low-income individuals. By being more self-sufficient, microcredit programs gain a better chance of weathering unforeseen fluctuations in funding cycles. In addition, programs that can generate their own incomes can potentially serve more clients. Stable programs with prospects for viability beyond the short term are more likely to win the community's trust. To facilitate a program's movement toward financial self-sufficiency, we suggest a multiproduct business strategy and an increased focus on operational efficiency.

First, expanding loan portfolios is a way to increase incomes without sacrificing services to low-income individuals. A program, for example, can develop a portfolio that includes both micro- and larger loans (say, those over $25,000). Since the overhead costs for larger loans are relatively smaller, incomes generated from larger loans can be used to cross-subsidize the "losses" incurred in making microloans. The experience of Arizona Multibank, a Community Development Corporation (CDC), provides some insights about such a strategy.

According to a report prepared by the Shorebank Advisory Services (1998), as of December 31, 1997, the CDC had provided 155 loans totaling $10.4 million, including 132 small-business loans totaling $5.5 million. Of these, 64 percent were microloans, representing 8 percent of total small-business dollars lent. On the other hand, larger loans in excess of $150,000 represented 8 percent of the loans made and 46 percent of the total.

dollars lent. Some may warn that operating a microcredit "window" within a lending institution that also disburses larger loans is nonviable in the long run, because of the inevitable clash between the different organizational cultures associated with the two different types of lending activities. Yet this strategy, at least in this case, supported "the CDC's commitment to make the smaller loans by offsetting the expense associated with the smaller, 'high touch' loan originations" (p. 10).

Second, to encourage operational efficiency of programs, sponsors of microcredit need to develop more-stringent operational standards regarding overhead costs per loan, number of loans disbursed per staff member, and perhaps most importantly, the time it takes for a borrower to receive funds. These standards must then be used consistently as benchmarks for evaluating organizational performance and making funding decisions.

In this regard, it is critical for sponsors to invest in building the capacity of microcredit programs and in providing them with technical assistance in instituting appropriate management and internal control systems. This involves assisting agencies on issues related to establishing appropriate governance structures, operating at optimal operational capacity, and planning for long-term portfolio growth. Building capacity in these areas may require providing training to agency personnel in conducting needs assessments, analyzing and approving loans, developing information systems for tracking repayments, and administering technical assistance and collections procedures for dealing with nonperforming loans.

One cannot overemphasize the importance of providing appropriate technical assistance to programs. Many microcredit initiatives have failed in the last decade because of inadequate management capacity and few internal controls. Lack of appropriate oversight,[5] including irresponsible decisions and actions by boards of directors, as well as inadequate performance and reporting standards, added to the problems of most agencies, which were often reluctant to reveal portfolio problems until it was too late.[6] Once clients perceived a program's management to be incompetent and lax, they became less likely to repay loans and more likely to abuse other services provided by the program. Sponsors need to recognize that assessing and building management capacity before and during project implementation are as critical as providing programs with funds for lending.

CONCLUSION

The argument that microenterprise development is key to inner-city revitalization has gained much currency in recent years. Many policy makers and development practitioners have advocated the creation of microcredit programs as a means of accomplishing a spectrum of objectives that range from poverty alleviation to economic development. Although microbusinesses may indeed help low-income people generate additional income and assets, and as a result, reduce their vulnerability to unexpected fluctuations in household income, a realistic appraisal of the inherent difficulties associated with running microcredit programs in the United States is warranted. As shown in our analysis, some microcredit programs in the United States have encountered major challenges in recruiting clients and in helping them build appropriate human capital; some have failed to manage risks and transaction costs; and some have been plagued with administrative inefficiencies. We have suggested that these challenges can potentially be addressed if programs develop appropriate lending techniques, financial products, non-financial services, and strategies for enhancing sustainability. However, since many of the strategies outlined are untested in the United States, more work needs to be done in evaluating the extent to which they are likely to enhance the viability of micro-credit programs.

This book has also emphasized the need for institutional analysis in designing microcredit policies and programs. Since a region's economy, laws, and customs combine in unique ways with the rules that govern individual and organizational interactions, a program "model" that gives rise to superior outcomes in one situation cannot be blindly replicated in another. This is because even where the rules are the same, the economic situation, the enforcement mechanism, and the ideology of the actors involved may well differ in subtle but important ways, making for considerable variation in the effectiveness of the institutions (Lin and Nugent, 1995).

In other words, the "quality of fit" achieved between a program's design features and a region's underlying economic, social, and administrative environments is critical to the viability of its institutions (Ostrom et al., 1993). The lackluster performance of many Third World microcredit replications in the United States has originated from a failure to account for factors such as the constraints faced by entrepreneurs in enterprise development, the contexts necessary for superior loan repayment performance, and the conditions which facilitate effective social, financial, and administrative intermediation. Indeed, it is inattention to the institutional dimensions of development that may have undermined the viability of many U.S. microcredit programs.

At a time when the development community around the world is desperately searching for strategies that are both people-centered and sustainable, microenterprise offers hope for enhancing incomes, assets, and employment opportunities in low-income communities. In this regard, microcredit may indeed be a promising vehicle for disbursing loans to those who possess the capacity, as well as the motivation, to realize their entrepreneurial potential. But transforming this vision into cost-effective policies and viable programs that can enhance the welfare of microentrepreneurs in the United States is a complex proposition. It requires policy makers, practitioners, and donors to focus not simply on replicating successful models, but on building viable institutions, keeping in mind the implications of a region's socioeconomic and institutional characteristics on program performance. Absent such a focus, microcredit programs, like many other development initiatives in the past, are unlikely to bear fruit.

NOTES

1. Although the Boston-based Working Capital has reportedly attained high levels of financial self-sufficiency through group-based lending, it is important to note that its major focus is not serving poor people who want to start businesses but rather serving existing entrepreneurs, many of whom belong to low-moderate income communities.

2. We owe this term to Vogel (1984).

3. Recent welfare-to-work grants to community-based agencies have recommended integration of IDAs in employment generation strategies. Although the implementation and integration of IDA initiatives with microlending programs have not yet achieved a broad scale, preliminary evaluations of pilot programs, conducted by the Center for Social Development at Washington University in St. Louis, reveal positive results.

4. Further, doing so will decrease programs' overhead costs and the risks of potential lender liability.

5. Taub's (1998) study of the Good Faith Fund in Arkansas underscores the importance of tight internal controls in microcredit programs. His examination of Good Faith Fund's high default rates between 1989 and 1992 (loan losses were 48 percent in 1989) revealed fraud by borrowers which was not noticed by management.

6. Bates (2000) suggests that inaccurate reporting of portfolio performance may be systemic within local economic development institu-

tions. He argues that this may be true not only for community-based programs but also for government agencies. For example, Bates (1994) reveals that losses incurred by SBA's economic opportunity loan program were 10 times higher than official SBA estimates.

Appendix:
Data Collection Methodology

R esearch data were collected from multiple sources to analyze the following: (a) microenterprise development constraints, (b) loan repayment performance, and (c) program sustainability.

(A) MICROENTERPRISE DEVELOPMENT CONSTRAINTS

The constraints faced by microentrepreneurs in obtaining financing and developing their enterprises were investigated by surveying 103 individuals who had been declined loans by banks within the last 12 months (chapter 3). Since most microcredit programs serve small-scale entrepreneurs who are likely to be excluded by the formal banking sector, selecting the aforementioned subjects was appropriate. But given the large numbers of such entrepreneurs, that is, those who had been denied bank loans, and the absence of any complete and reliable database that captured the names and addresses of their enterprises, a random sampling of the entire population was difficult. Therefore, for the purposes of this study, entrepreneurs who had approached three microenterprise development programs in California for assistance were surveyed. These three programs were the Neighborhood Entrepreneurship Program, Community Enterprise Program, and Enterprise Development Corporation.

The survey instrument was pretested with NEP program participants in October 1997, and was adjusted based on the feedback received. Although the survey contained eight questions that asked for information about the respondent's enterprise, ability to obtain financing from formal and informal sources, reasons for being denied bank loans, and various factors that hindered the respondent in developing a business, only responses to four questions were directly related to specific hypotheses. The other four questions served to provide additional information on the entrepreneurs and their ventures, which assisted in the formulation of additional queries/questions that were asked of the focus group participants. A four-point Likert-type scale was constructed to measure entrepreneurs' responses to questions that asked "to what extent" various factors hindered their ability to develop their businesses and access capital. Response categories ranged from 4 (strongly hindered) to 1 (did not hinder at all). Questions regarding the entrepreneur's socioeconomic characteristics such as education, gender, and ethnicity were also included in the survey.

The surveys were distributed to agency program officers who had their clients complete them during the January–March 1998 period. Seventeen Hispanic, 26 Caucasian, 19 Asian American, and 41 African American entrepreneurs filled out complete surveys. In addition to the above surveys, two focus group sessions were conducted at CEP and EDC during the third week of May 1998. Sixteen participants were selected based on their responses to the completed questionnaires. Out of this group, eight entrepreneurs indicated that they were capital-constrained because of the various factors mentioned in the survey instrument, while the other eight did not feel constrained. A total of 16 entrepreneurs were asked various questions about what factors served as the major constraints in developing their enterprises and accessing capital.

(B) LOAN REPAYMENT PERFORMANCE

In order to study the determinants of loan repayment, the borrower and program characteristics, as well as repayment records of four microcredit programs—Neighborhood Entrepreneurship Program, First Chance, Women's Development Association, and Community Enterprise Program—were analyzed (chapter 4).

While NEP provided us with direct access to client files, the other three agencies denied such access, claiming that the information was proprietary in nature and, as such, could not be accessed by the public. WDA management did, however, make limited financial information available to us from the agency's archives.

The directors and/or program managers of these agencies let us examine pertinent and selected information from client files, including loan repayment records for group borrowers. In WDA's case, agency data for the first three years of operation were not collected in any standardized format. Also, since the agency was "wrapping up" its operations and client files were being sent back to the funders when we made the request for borrower data, such information could not be accessed. As a result, additional socio-economic and other background information on the borrowers could not be accessed for the study.

Information on the following six borrower characteristics was provided by all four programs: (1) the borrower's gender, (2) the borrower's educational level, (3) the borrower's household income, (4) the degree of formality of the borrower's business, indicated by the presence or absence of a business license, (5) the number of years that the borrower had been in business, and

(6) the proximity of the borrower's business to the lending agency. This information was used to analyze the socioeconomic determinants of loan repayment.

In order to assess the institutional determinants of loan repayment, another survey was designed to gather information about the personal- and enterprise-level characteristics of NEP borrowers. Not all questions asked were directly related to the hypotheses tested in chapter 4; some questions served to provide a broader view of the various lending and borrowing processes and their impacts, including how institutional factors such as transaction costs, borrower homogeneity, and the threat of sanctions impacted loan repayment performance.

Since the borrowers surveyed did not have any active loans, and since many had taken out loans that were ultimately written off, a number of questions at the beginning of the survey instrument were designed to provide the respondent with a comfortable setting for answering the questions that followed. Further, these questions served to facilitate recall for the questions that followed. In order to assess the transaction costs incurred by borrowers, a four-point Likert-type scale was constructed to measure responses to items that asked the respondents "to what extent" they considered the program's various activities to be convenient and efficient. Response categories ranged from 4 (do not agree) to 1 (strongly agree). Some of the eight response items included the waiting time to participate in training, length of training, and availability and flexibility of program staff.

To assess the level of group homogeneity, and the extent to which it impacted loan repayment, eight specific response-items were formulated to measure the trait and preference homogeneity index of a member's group. The questions were an adaptation of factors employed by Hemphill (1956, cited in Miller, 1991, p. 366) in creating the Group Homogeneity Indices. Finally, in order to gain insight into the extent to which a borrower perceived that loan default would result in sanctions by the community or the program, borrowers were asked the question "What did you think would happen if you did not repay the loan?"

The survey instrument was first pretested in November 1997. Based on the responses and the qualitative feedback received, appropriate adjustments were made to the design of the instrument. A first attempt to survey participants was made at NEP's New Year Holiday Reception in December 1997. Only four participants showed up for this event. During the following two weeks, the survey was mailed out to all 54 borrowers, and a sum of $15 was offered as an incentive for returning the completed survey—in an enclosed, stamped return envelope—within two weeks. Phone calls were made to follow up and remind individuals to mail back the survey. This led to the return of 18 surveys. Subsequent to this deadline, another round of surveys was sent out, and the reward sum was increased to $25. Another four surveys were received, increasing the total number of completed surveys equal to 26, which accounted for 50 percent of the total population of 54 borrowers.

Further, during the months of February and March 1998, four in-depth focus group interviews were conducted with ten selected borrowers, as well as program staff, management, and board members of all programs, to gain a deeper insight into the factors affecting program performance. No incentives were offered to those who participated in these sessions.

(C) PROGRAM SUSTAINABILITY

Data regarding portfolio at risk and loan losses for the Women's Development Association program (chapter 5) were made available to us by program staff.

References

Adams, D. W., and J. D. Von Pischke. 1992. Microenterprise credit programs: deja vu? *World Development* 20 (10), 1463–1470.

Adams, D. W., D. H. Graham, and J. D. Von Pischke. 1984. *Undermining rural development with cheap credit.* Boulder, CO: Westview Press.

Aldrich, H., and C. Zimmer. 1985. Entrepreneurship through social networks. In D. L. Sexton and R. W. Smilor (eds.), *The art and science of entrepreneurship* (pp. 3–24). Cambridge, MA: Ballinger Publishing Company.

Aldrich, J. H., and F. D. Nelson. 1984. *Linear probability, logit, and probit models.* London and New Delhi: Sage.

Anthony, D. L., and S. Smith. 1996. Working capital: helping small business work—preliminary results of initial impact assessment. Paper presented at the Association for Enterprise Opportunity Conference in Providence, Rhode Island, May 1–4.

Ashe, J. 1985. *The PISCES II experience: local efforts in micro-enterprise development.* Washington, DC: United States Agency for International Development.

Aspen Institute. 1999. *1999 Directory of U.S. Microenterprise Programs.* Washington, DC: The Aspen Institute.

Auwal, M. A. 1996. Promoting microcapitalism in service of the poor: The Grameen model and its cross-cultural adaptation. *Journal of Business Communication* 33 (1), 27–49.

Balkin, S. 1989a. *Self-employment for low income people: a report to the national commission on jobs and small business.* Springfield, VA: U.S. Department of Commerce.

Balkin, S. 1989b. *Self-employment for low-income people*. New York: Praeger.

Barenbach, S., and D. Guzman. 1994. The solidarity group experience worldwide. In M. Otero and E. Rhyne (eds.), *The new world of microenterprise finance* (pp. 119–132). West Hartford, CT: Kumarian Press.

Barreto, H. 1989. *The entrepreneur in microeconomics: disappearance and explanation*. London: Routledge.

Barringer, P. 1993. Microenterprise development. *Economic Development Commentary, Fall*, 4–11.

Bates, T. 1994. Social resources generated by group support networks may not be beneficial to Asian immigrant-owned small businesses. *Social Forces* 72 (3), 671–689.

Bates. T. 1995. A bad investment. *Inc.* 17 (1), 27.

Bates, T. 1997. *Race, self-employment, and upward mobility: an illusive American dream*. Baltimore: Johns Hopkins Press.

Bates, T. 2000. Financing the development of urban minority communities. *Economic Development Quarterly* 14, 227–241.

Bates, T., and L. J. Servon. 1996. Why loans won't save the poor. *Inc.* 18 (5), 27–28.

Bender, A. D., J. T. Meli, L. K. Turnbull, W. C. Payne, and C. E. Russell. 1990. Entrepreneurship education and microbusiness development as part of a program of community revitalization. *Economic Development Review* 8 (1), 38–41.

Bennett, L., and M. Goldberg. 1993. *Providing enterprise development and financial services to women: a decade of bank experience in Asia*. Washington, DC: The World Bank.

Benus, J. M., T. P. Johnson, M. Wood, N. Grover, and T. Shen. 1995. Self-employment programs: a new reemployment strategy, Final report on the UI Self-employment Demonstration. Unemployment Insurance Occasional Paper 95-4. Washington, DC: U.S. Department of Labor.

Berman, E., and J. D. Jurie. 1998. Community building and economic development. In T. Liou (ed.), *Handbook of economic development* (pp. 283–300). New York: Marcel Dekker, Inc.

Besley, T. 1995. Nonmarket institutions for credit and risk sharing in low-income countries. *Journal of Economic Perspectives* 9 (3), 115–127.

Besley, T., and S. Coate. 1995. Group lending, repayment incentives and social collateral. *Journal of Development Economics* 46, 1–18.

Bhatt, E. 1998. A bank of one's own. *Consultative Group to Assist the Poorest, Newsletter 5*. Washington, DC: The World Bank.

Bhatt, N. 1997. Microenterprise development and the entrepreneurial poor: including the excluded? *Public Administration and Development* 17, 371–386.

Bhatt, N. 1998. Capacity building for microenterprise development. *International Journal of Technical Cooperation* 4, 69–82.

Bhatt, N. 2000. Alleviating poverty in the global metropolis: The social enterprise promise. Paper prepared for the 51st Annual Council on Foundations Conference, May 1–3, 2000, Los Angeles, California.

Bhatt, N., and S. Y. Tang. 1998a. The problem of transaction costs in group-based microlending: an institutional perspective. *World Development* 32 (4), 623–637.

Bhatt, N., and S. Y. Tang. 1998b. Group-based microfinance and economic development. In T. Liou (ed.), *Handbook of economic development* (pp. 115–138). New York: Marcel Dekker.

Bhatt, N., and S. Y. Tang. Forthcoming. Delivering microfinance in developing countries: controversies and policy perspectives. *Policy Studies Journal*.

Bhatt, N., and Y. S. P. Thorat. 2001. India's Regional Rural Banks: the institutional dimension of reforms. *Journal of Microfinance* 3(1), 65–94.

Bhatt, N., G. Painter, and S. Y. Tang. 1999a. Can microcredit work in the US? *Harvard Business Review*, November/December.

Bhatt, N., G. Painter, and S. Y. Tang. 1999b. Microcredit programs in the US: the challenges of outreach and sustainability. Paper prepared for the Twenty-first Annual Research Conference on Public Policy Analysis and Management, November 4–6, Washington, DC.

Birley, S. 1987. New ventures and employment growth. *Journal of Business Venturing* 1, 107–117.

Bonavoglia, A. 2000. *Women's work: asset building and community development*. New York: Ford Foundation.

Borjas, G. J. 1986. The self-employment experience of immigrants. *The Journal of Human Resources* XXI (4), 485–506.

Bracker, J. S. 1993. A note on starting an entrepreneurial business through venture capital. In D. F. Jennings (ed.), *Multiple perspectives on entrepreneurship* (pp. 303–314). Cincinnati, OH: South-Western Publishing Co.

Buntin, J. 1997. Bad credit: microcredit yields macroproblems. *The New Republic* (March), 10–11.

Burrus, W. 1997. A little credit can go a long way. *Credit World* 85 (5), 18–20.

Burrus, W., and K. Stearn. 1997. *Building a model: ACCION's approach to microenterprise in the United States*. Washington, DC: ACCION International.

Buvinic, M., M. Berger, and C. Jaramillo. 1989. Impact of a credit project for women and men microentrepreneurs in Quito, Ecuador. In M. Berger and M. Buvinic (eds.), *Women's Ventures* (pp. 222–246). West Hartford, CT: Kumarian Press.

Caskey, J. P. 1994. *Fringe banking: check-cashing outlets, pawnshops and the poor*. New York: Russell Sage Foundation.

Casson, M. 1982. *The entrepreneur: an economic theory*. New Jersey: Noble Publishers.

CGAP (Consultative Group to Assist the Poorest). 1997. Impact assessment methodologies: report of a virtual meeting, April 7–19. Washington, DC: The World Bank.

Chami, R., and J. H. Fischer. 1995. Community banking, monitoring, and the Clinton plan. *Cato Journal* 14 (3), 493–508.

Christen, M. 1997. *Banking services for the poor: managing for financial success*. Washington, DC: ACCION International.

Christen, M., H. S. Lecomte, and X. Oudin. 1994. *Microenterprises and the institutional framework in developing countries*. Paris: OECD.

Christen, R. P. 1992. Formal credit for informal borrowers: lessons from informal lenders. In D. W. Adams and D. A. Fitchett (eds.), *Informal finance in low-income countries* (pp. 281–292). Oxford: Westview Press.

Christen, R. P., E. Rhyne, and R. C. Vogel. 1994. *Maximizing the outreach of microenterprise finance: the emerging lessons of successful programs*. Washington, DC: IMCC.

Clark, P., and A. Kays. 1999. *Microenterprise and the poor: findings from the self-employment learning project*. Washington, DC: The Aspen Institute.

Coleman, J. S. 1988. Social capital in the creation of human capital. *American Journal of Sociology* 94, S95–S120.

Coleman, J. S. 1993. The rational reconstruction of society. *American Sociological Review* 58, 1–15.

Cooper, A. C., and F. J. G. Gascon. 1992. Entrepreneurs, processes of founding and new-firm performance. In D. L. Sexton and J. D. Kasarda (eds.), *The state of the art of entrepreneurship* (pp. 301–340). Boston, MA: PWS-KENT.

Counts, A. 1996. *Give us credit: how Muhammad Yunus's micro-lending revolution is empowering women from Bangladesh to Chicago.* New York: Times Books.

Davis, B. 1995. A practical guide to creating a revolving loan fund. *Management Quarterly* 36 (1), 24–40.

Day, D. L. 1992. Research linkages between entrepreneurship and strategic management or general management. In D. L. Sexton and J. D. Kasarda (eds.), *The state of the art of entrepreneurship* (pp. 117–163). Boston, MA: PWS-KENT.

de Soto, H. 1989. *The other path: the invisible revolution in the Third World.* New York: Harper and Row.

Desai, B. M. 1982. *Group lending innovation for rural areas: a pilot study.* New Delhi: IBH Publishing Company.

Devereux, S., and M. Fishe. 1993. An economic analysis of group lending in developing countries. *Developing Economies* 31 (1), 102–121.

Dichter, T. W. 1996. Questioning the future of NGOs in microfinance. *Journal of International Development* 8 (2), 259–269.

Dreier, P. 1991. Redlining cities: how banks color community development. *Challenge* (November–December), 15–23.

Drury, D., S. Walsh, and M. Strong. 1994. Evaluation of the EDWAA job creation demonstration. Research and evaluation report series 94-G. U.S. Department of Labor, Employment and Training Administration. Office of Policy and Research, Washington, DC.

Dymski, G. A. 1993. The theory of bank redlining and discrimination: an exploration. *The Review of Black Political Economy* (Winter), 38–74.

Dymski, G. A. 1996. Business strategy and access to capital in inner-city revitalization. *Review of Black Political Economy* 24 (2/3), 51–65.

Dymski, G. A., and J. M. Veitch. 1991. It's not a wonderful life: bank lending for affordable housing in Los Angeles. Working Paper, Department of Economics, University of California at Riverside.

Dymski, G. A., and J. M. Veitch. 1996. Financing the future in Los Angeles: from depression to 21st century. In M. J. Dear, H. E. Schockman and G. Hise (eds.), *Rethinking Los Angeles* (pp. 35–55). Thousand Oaks, CA: Sage.

Edgcomb, E., J. Klein, and P. Clark. 1996. *The practice of microenterprise in the U.S.* Washington, DC: The Aspen Institute.

Eggertsson, T. 1990. *Economic behavior and institutions.* New York: Cambridge University Press.

Ehlers, T. B., and K. Main. 1998. Pink collar businesses: the false promise of microenterprise. *Gender and Society* 12 (4), 424–440.

Else, J. F., and C. Clay-Thompson. 1998. *Refugee microenterprise development: achievements and lessons learned.* Iowa City: Institute for Social and Economic Development.

Else, J. F., and S. Raheim. 1992. AFDC clients as entrepreneurs: self-employment offers an important option. *Public Welfare* 50 (4), 36–41.

Eswaran, M., and A. Kotwal. 1986. Access to capital and agrarian production organization. *The Economic Journal* 96, 482–498.

Evans, D., and L. S. Leighton. 1990. Small business formation by unemployed and employed workers. *Small Business Economics* 2 (4), 12–24.

Feder, G. 1990. The relationship between credit and productivity in Chinese agriculture: a microeconomic model of disequilibrium. *American Journal of Agricultural Economics* (December), 1151–1157.

Fettig, D. 1996. Rethinking community economic development. *Fedgazette* 8 (1), 5–6.

Fratoe, F. A. 1988. Social capital of black business owners. *The Review of Black Political Economy* 16, 33–50.

Friedman, R. E., B. Grossman, and P. Sahay. 1995. *Building assets: self-employment for welfare recipients.* Washington, DC: Corporation for Enterprise Development.

Fry, M. J. 1995. *Money, interest and banking in economic development.* Baltimore, MD: The Johns Hopkins University Press.

Furubotn, E. G., and R. Richter. 1997. *Institutions and economic theory: the contribution of the new institutional economics*. Ann Arbor: The University of Michigan Press.

Giles, J. C. 1993. Microbusiness lending: bank services for the smallest companies. *Journal of Commercial Lending* 76 (3), 21–31.

Goldsmith, W. W., and E. J. Blakely. 1992. *Separate societies*. Philadelphia, PA: Temple University Press.

Gonzalez-Vega, C., M. Schreiner, R. L. Meyer, J. Rodriguez, and S. Navajas. 1997. BancoSol: the challenge of growth for microfinance organizations. In H. Schneider (ed.), *Microfinance for the poor?* (pp. 109–128). Paris: OECD.

Greenwald, B. C., and J. E. Stiglitz. 1990. Asymmetric information and the new theory of the firm: financial constraints and risk behavior. *The American Economic Review* 80 (2), 160–165.

Grenell, K. D. 1998. Private entrepreneurship and grassroots development strategies. In T. Liou (ed.), *Handbook of economic development* (pp. 337–353). New York: Marcel Dekker.

Grosh, B., and G. Somolekae. 1996. Mighty oaks from little acorns: can microenterprise serve as the seedbed of industrialization? *World Development* 24 (12), 1879–1890.

Grzywinski, R., R. P. Taub, and E. Reardon. 1992. Capital and the promotion of entrepreneurship in the rural United States. In *Business and jobs in the rural world* (pp. 75–84). Paris: Organization for Economic Cooperation and Development.

Gunn, C., and H. D. Gunn. 1991. *Reclaiming capital: democratic initiatives and community development*. Ithaca: Cornell University Press.

Himes, C., with L. J. Servon. 1998. *Measuring client success: an evaluation of ACCION's impact on microenterprises in the United States*. The U.S. Issues Series No. 2. Washington, DC: ACCION International.

Holt, S. L. 1994. The village bank methodology: performance and prospect. In M. Otero and E. Rhyne (eds.), *The new world of microenterprise finance: building healthy financial institutions for the poor* (pp. 156–184). West Hartford, CT: Kumarian Press.

Hossain, M. 1988. *Credit for the alleviation of rural poverty: The Grameen Bank in Bangladesh*. Washington, DC: International Food Policy Institute.

Hulme, D., and P. Mosley. 1996. *Finance against poverty, Vol. 1*. London: Routledge.

Hulme, D., R. Montgomery, and D. Bhattacharya. 1994. Mutual finance and the poor: a study of the Federation of Thrift and Credit Cooperatives in Sri Lanka (SANASA). Working Paper No. 11. Institute for Development Policy and Management, Department of Economics, Reading University.

Huppi, M., and G. Feder. 1990. The role of groups and credit cooperatives in rural lending. *The World Bank Research Observer* 5 (2), 187–204.

International Labour Organization. 1997. *Collateral, collateral law and collateral substitutes*. Enterprise and Cooperative Development Department. Geneva: ILO.

Jani, N. D., and M. N. Pedroni. 1997. Financing women entrepreneurs in South Asia: a conversation with Nancy Barry. *Journal of International Affairs* 51 (1), 169–178.

Johnson, M. A. 1998. An overview of basic issues facing microenterprise practices in the United States. *Journal of Developmental Entrepreneurship* 3 (1), 5–21.

Jordon, J. L. 1993. Community lending and economic development. *Economic Commentary* (November), 1–4.

Khandker, S. R. 1996. Grameen Bank: impact, costs and program sustainability. *Asian Development Review* 14 (1), 97–130.

Khandker, S. R. 1998. *Fighting poverty with microcredit: experience in Bangladesh*. New York: Oxford University Press.

Khandker, S. R., B. Khalily, and Z. Khan. 1995. *Grameen Bank: performance and sustainability*. Washington, DC: The World Bank.

Korten, D. C. 1990. *Getting to the 21st century: voluntary action and the global agenda*. West Hartford, CT: Kumarian Press.

Laguerre, M. 1998. Rotating credit associations and the diasporic economy. *Journal of Developmental Entrepreneurship* 3 (1), 23–34.

Light, I. 1972. *Ethnic enterprise in America: business and welfare among Chinese, Japanese and Blacks*. Berkeley, CA: The University of California Press.

Light, I. 1998. Microcredit and informal credit in the USA: new strategies of economic development. *Journal of Developmental Entrepreneurship* 3 (1), 1–4.

Light, I., and E. Bonacich. 1988. *Immigrant entrepreneurs: Koreans in Los Angeles, 1965–1982*. Berkeley, CA: The University of California Press.

Light, I., and M. Pham. 1998. Beyond creditworthy: microcredit and informal credit in the United States. *Journal of Developmental Entrepreneurship* 3 (1), 1–4.

Light, I., P. Bhachu, and S. Karageorgis. 1993. Migration networks and immigrant entrepreneurship. In I. Light and P. Bhachu (eds.), *Immigration and entrepreneurship: culture, capital and ethnic networks* (pp. 25–50). New Brunswick, NJ, and London: Transaction Publishers.

Lin, J. Y., and J. B. Nugent. 1995. Institutions and economic development. In J. Behrman and T. N. Srinivasan (eds.) *The handbook of economic development* (pp. 2301–2368). Amsterdam: North-Holland.

Male, C. 1993. Women's issues related to microenterprises and the informal sector. In *New directions in donor assistance to microenterprises* (pp. 35–42). Paris: OECD.

Mead, L. M. 1989. The hidden jobs debate. *Public Interest* 91, 40–58.

Miller, D. C. 1991. *Handbook of research design and social measurement*. Newbury Park, CA: Sage.

Min, P. G. 1993. Korean immigrants in Los Angeles. In I. Light and P. Bhachu (eds.), *Immigration and entrepreneurship: culture, capital and ethnic networks* (pp. 185–204). New Brunswick, NJ, and London: Transaction Publishers.

Morduch, J. 1998. Does microfinance really help the poor? New evidence from flagship programs in Bangladesh. Paper presented at the Seminar in Aging, Development, and Population, July 2, at the RAND Corporation, Santa Monica, CA.

Morduch, J. 1999. The microfinance promise. *Journal of Economic Literature* XXXVII, 1569–1614.

Morduch, J. 2000. The microfinance schism. *World Development*, 28 (4), 617–629.

Morrisson, C., H. S. Lecomte, and X. Oudin. 1994. *Microenterprises and the institutional framework in developing countries*. Paris: OECD.

NAPA (National Academy of Public Administration). 1996. *A path to smarter economic development: reassessing the federal role*. Washington, DC: NAPA.

Navajas, S., M. Schreiner, R. Meyer, C. Gonzalez-Vega, and J. Rodriguez-Meza. 2000. Microfinance and the poorest of the poor: theory and evidence from Bolivia. *World Development* 28 (2), 333–346.

Nelson, C. 1994. *Going forward: the peer group lending exchange: a report on the conference.* Toronto: Calmeadow.

New York Times. 1999. A grand idea that went badly awry. 14 November, Sunday, Late Edition – Final.

North, D. 1990. *Institutions, institutional change and economic performance.* New York: Cambridge University Press.

O'Regan, F., and M. Conway. 1993. *From the bottom up: toward a strategy for income and employment generation among the disadvantaged.* Washington, DC: The Aspen Institute.

Ostrom, E. 1990. *Governing the commons: the evolution of institutions for collective action.* New York: Cambridge University Press.

Ostrom, E. 1997. Self-governance of common-pool resources. Working Paper, Workshop in Political Theory and Policy Analysis, Indiana University, Bloomington, IN.

Ostrom, E. 1998. A behavioral approach to the rational-choice theory of collective action. Working Paper, Workshop in Political Theory and Policy Analysis, Indiana University, Bloomington, IN.

Ostrom, E., L. Schroeder, and S. Wynne. 1993. *Institutional incentives and sustainable development: infrastructure policies in perspective.* Boulder, CO: Westview Press.

Otero, M., and E. Rhyne. 1994. *The new world of microenterprise finance: building healthy financial institutions for the poor.* West Hartford, CT: Kumarian Press.

Price, C., and S. Monroe. 1991. Educational training for women and minority entrepreneurs positively impacts venture growth and development. Paper presented at the Babson Entrepreneurship Research Conference, Houston, Texas.

Putnam, R. 1993a. *Making democracy work: civic traditions in modern Italy.* Princeton, NJ: Princeton University Press.

Putnam, R. 1993b. The prosperous community: social capital and public life. *The American Prospect* 13, 35–42.

Raheim, S. 1996. Microenterprise as an approach to promoting economic development in social work. *International Social Work* 39 (1), 68–82.

Raheim, S. 1997. Problems and prospects of self-employment as an economic independence option for welfare recipients. *Social Work* 42 (1), 44–53.

Raheim, S., and C. F. Alter. 1995. Self-employment investment demonstration: final evaluation report. Washington, DC: Corporation for Enterprise Development.

Raheim, S., and C. F. Alter. 1998. Self-employment as a social and economic development intervention for recipients of AFDC. *Journal of Community Practice* 5 (1/2), 41–61.

Raheim, S., C. F. Alter, and D. Yarbrough. 1996. Evaluating microenterprise programs: issues and lessons learned. *Journal of Developmental Entrepreneurship* 1 (2), 87–103.

Rhyne, E. 1994. A new view of finance program evaluation. In M. Otero and E. Rhyne (eds.), *The new world of microenterprise finance: building healthy financial institutions for the poor* (pp. 105–116). West Hartford, CT: Kumarian Press.

Robinson, M. 1996. Addressing some key questions on finance and poverty. *Journal of International Development* 8 (2), 153–161.

Rodriguez, C. R. 1995. *Women, microenterprise and the politics of self-help.* New York: Garland Publishing, Inc.

Rothbart, R. 1993. The ethnic saloon as a form of immigrant enterprise. *International Migration Review* XXVII, 332–357.

Sage, G. 1993. Entrepreneurship as an economic development strategy. *Economic Development Review, Spring,* 66–67.

Sanders, J. M., and V. Nee. 1996. Immigrant self-employment: the family as social capital and the value of human capital. *American Sociological Review* 61 (April), 231–249.

Schreiner, M. 1998. The context for microenterprises and for microenterprise programs in the United States and abroad. Manuscript. Washington University in St. Louis. gwbweb.wustl.edu/users/schreiner/.

Schreiner, M. 1999a. Lessons for microenterprise programs from the Unemployment Insurance Self-Employment Demonstration. *Evaluation Review* 23 (5), 503–526.

Schreiner, M. 1999b. A cost-effectiveness analysis of the Grameen Bank of Bangladesh. Working Paper No. 99-5. Center for Social Development, Washington University.

Schreiner, M. 1999c. A review of evaluations of microenterprise programs in the United States. Manuscript. Washington University in St. Louis. gwbweb.wustl.edu/users/schreiner/.

Schreiner, M. 1999d. Self-employment, microenterprise, and the poorest. *Social Services Review* 73 (4), 496–523.

Schuler, S. R., and S. M. Hashemi. 1994. Credit programs, women's empowerment and contraceptive use in Bangladesh. *Studies in Family Planning* 25 (2), 65–76.

Schultz, T. 1975. The value of the ability to deal with disequilibria. *Journal of Economic Literature* 13, 827–846.

Schumpeter, J. A. [1934] 1974. *The theory of economic development.* Translated by Redvers Opie. Reprinted London, Oxford University Press.

Scott, C. E. 1986. Why more women are becoming entrepreneurs. *Journal of Small Business Management* 24 (4), 37–44.

Servon, L. J. 1997. Microenterprise in the U.S. inner cities: economic development or social welfare? *Economic Development Quarterly* 11 (2), 166–180.

Servon, L. J. 1999. *Bootstrap capital: microenterprises and the American poor.* Washington, DC: Brookings Institution Press.

Servon, L. J., and T. Bates. 1998. Microenterprise as an exit route from poverty: recommendations for programs and policy makers. *Journal of Urban Affairs* 20 (4), 419–441.

Sethi, R., and E. Somanathan. 1996. The evolution of social norms in common property resource use. *American Economic Review* 86 (4), 766–788.

Sharma, M., and M. Zeller. 1997. Repayment performance in group-based credit programs in Bangladesh: an empirical analysis. *World Development* 25 (10), 1731–1742.

Sherraden, M. 1991. *Assets and the poor: a new American welfare policy.* M. E. Sharpe: New York.

Shorebank Advisory Services. 1998. *Guidelines for establishing multi-bank community development corporations.* Report prepared for Nations Bank Community Investment Group.

Sirola, P. 1992. Beyond survival: Latino immigrant street vendors in the Los Angeles informal sector. Paper prepared for the XVII International Congress of the Latin American Studies Association, Los Angeles, CA, September.

Solomon, L. D. 1992. Microenterprise: human reconstruction in America's inner cities. *Harvard Journal of Law and Public Policy* 15 (1), 191–222.

Spalter-Roth, R. M., E. Soto, and L. Zandiniapour. 1994. *Microenterprise and women: the viability of self-employment as a strategy for alleviating poverty.* Washington, DC: Institute for Women's Policy Research.

Sterns, K. 1991. *Interest rates and self-sufficiency.* GEMINI Technical Note. New York: ACCION International.

Stiglitz, J. E. 1987. Economic organization, information and development. In H. Chenery and T. N. Srinivasan (eds.), *Handbook of development economics,* Vol. 1 (pp. 213–233). Amsterdam: North Holland.

Stiglitz, J. E. 1990. Peer monitoring and credit markets. *World Bank Economic Review* 4, 351–366.

Stiglitz, J. E., and A. Weiss. 1983. Incentive effects of terminations: applications to the credit and labor markets. *American Economic Review* 72, 912–927.

Stoesz, D., and D. Saunders. 1999. Welfare capitalism: a new approach to poverty policy? *Social Service Review* (September), 380–400.

Stuart, R., and P. A. Abetti. 1986. Field studies of start-up ventures, Part 2: predicting initial success. In R. Ronstadt, J. Hornaday, R. Peterson and K. Vesper (eds.), *Frontiers of entrepreneurship research* (pp. 21–39). Wellesley, MA.: Babson College.

Tang, S. Y. 1992. *Institutions and collective action.* San Francisco, CA: ICS Press.

Taub, R. P. 1998. Making the adaptation across cultures and societies: a report on an attempt to clone the Grameen Bank in South Arkansas. *Journal of Development Entrepreneurship* 3 (1), 53–69.

Tella, G. 1969. The behavior of the firm with a financial repression. *The Journal of Industrial Economics,* XVII (2), 119–131.

Timmons, J. A. 1985. *New venture creation,* 2nd Edition. Homewood, IL: Richard D. Irwin, Inc.

Tsukashima, R. T. 1991. Cultural endowment, disadvantaged status and economic niche: the development of an ethnic trade. *International Migration Review* 25 (2), 333–354.

U.S. Government. 1995. *Revitalizing America's rural and urban communities*. Hearing before the committee on small business, United States Senate. 104th Congress, First session. October 19, 1995.

Varian, H. R. 1990. Monitoring agents with agents. *Journal of Institutional and Theoretical Economics* 146, 153–179.

Vesper, K. H. 1980. *New venture strategies*. New Jersey: Prentice Hall, Inc.

Vogel, R. C. 1984. Savings mobilization: the forgotten half of rural finance. In D. W. Adams, D. H. Graham and J. D. von Pischke (eds.), *Undermining rural development with cheap credit*. Boulder, CO: Westview Press.

Von Pischke, J. D. 1991. *Finance at the frontier: debt capacity and the role of credit in the private economy*. Washington, DC: The World Bank.

Von Pischke, J. D. 1999. Reaching the poor: microfinance in developing countries. Paper prepared for the 21st Annual Research Conference of the Association of Public Policy Analysis and Management. November 4–6.

Von Pischke, J. D., H. Schneider, and R. Zander. 1997. Introductory overview: principles and perspectives. In H. Schneider (ed.), *Microfinance for the poor?* (pp. 9–42). Paris: OECD.

Wahid, A. N. M. 1994. The Grameen Bank and poverty alleviation in Bangladesh: theory, evidence and limitations. *The American Journal of Economics and Sociology* 52 (1), 1–15.

Waldinger, R. 1986. *Through the eye of the needle: immigrant enterprise in New York's garment trades*. New York: New York University Press.

Waldinger, R. 1995. The 'other side' of embeddnessness: a case-study of the interplay of economy and ethnicity. *Ethnic and Racial Studies* 18 (3), 555–580.

Wells, M. 1991. Ethnic groups and knowledge system in agriculture. *Economic Development and Cultural Change* 39, 739–771.

Williamson, O. E. 1985. *The economic institutions of capitalism*. New York: Free Press.

Woller, G., C. Dunford, and W. Woodworth. 1999. Where to microfinance? *International Journal of Economic Development* 1 (1). (www.spaef.com/IJED_PUB/v1n1.html).

Women's World Banking. 1993. Best practice training. *What Works* 3 (1).

World Bank 1996. *The World Bank participation sourcebook*. Washington, DC: The World Bank.

World Bank 1997. *Burkina Faso: le projet de promotion du petit credit rural*. Sustainable Banking for the Poor. Washington, DC: The World Bank.

Yaron, J. 1992. *Assessing development finance institutions: a public interest analysis*. Washington, DC: The World Bank.

Yaron, J. 1994. What makes rural finance institutions successful? *The World Bank Research Observer* 9 (1), 49–70.

Yaron, J., M. Benjamin, and S. Charitonenko. 1998. Promoting efficient rural financial intermediation. *The World Bank Research Observer* 13 (2), 147–170.

Yinger, J. 1998. Evidence of discrimination in consumer markets. *Journal of Economic Perspectives* 12 (2), 23–40.

Yoon, I. 1991. The changing significance of ethnic and class resources in immigrant businesses: the case of Korean immigrant businesses in Chicago. *International Migration Review* 25, 303–331.

Yuengert, A. M. 1992. Testing hypotheses of immigrant self-employment. *The Journal of Human Resources*, XXX (1), 194–204.

Yunus, M. 1991. Grameen Bank: some thoughts and experiences. Paper prepared for the conference on the Economic Advancement of Rural Women in Asia and the Pacific, September 15–21, 1991, Kuala Lampur, Malaysia.

Yunus, M. 1995. The value of microenterprise development. Statement and hearing before the U.S. Committee on International Relations, House of Representatives, 104th Congress, First session, June 27, 1995. Washington, DC: U. S. Government Printing Office.

Zeller, M. 1998. Determinants of repayment performance in credit groups: the role of program design, intragroup risk pooling and social cohesion. *Economic Development and Cultural Change* 46 (3), 599–620.

Index

ACCION International, 3, 7, 10,
    23n.19, 31, 102, 114n.13, 118,
    120, 132–33n.3, 141, 143, 144
ACCION San Antonio, 105
Administration, 43, 138–39
    practices of, 127–32
Administrative intermediation, 127,
    138–39
Advocacy groups, 143
African Americans, 17, 18, 55, 56, 160
    constraints on, 71, 74, 75
    social networks of, 63, 67
Arizona Multibank, 152–53
Armenians, 17
Asians, 17, 55, 67–68, 71, 160
Aspen Institute, 10
Assessment
    of borrowers' success, 25–28
    of business opportunities, 147–48
Assets, 75, 146

BancoSol, 3, 105
Bangladesh, 3, 27, 45n.5, 99
Banking, banks, 21–22nn. 13, 15, 49,
    74
    lender proximity and, 95–96, 111,
        113n.7
    lending criteria of, 57–58
    redlining by, 56–57
"Begin-a-Biz" curriculum, 121–22
Bolivia, 105
Borrowers, 58, 98

individual, 85–86
loan losses and, 89–90
and program assessment, 25–26
and program efficiency, 32–33
Burkina Faso, 98
Business licenses, 37
Business opportunities: assessing,
    147–48
Businesses, 78n.1, 80n.9
    development of, 120–21
    feasibility of, 69–70
    formality of, 91–92
    loans to, 140–41
    poor, 26–27

California, 7
    Japanese American gardeners in,
        61–62
    loan denial in, 118–19
    microcredit programs in, 11, 16–18
    microenterprise programs in,
        159–61
    microenterprise socioeconomics in,
        64–66
    NEP loans in, 99–101
    outreach, 117, 118
Capacity building, 141–42
Capital, 14, 47, 79n.5, 132–33n.3, 139
    microentrepreneurial use of, 34, 37
    and cash flow, 48–49
    constraints on, 49–50, 60, 67,
        73(table)

Capital (*continued*)
  lack of, 50–52
  access to, 55, 56–63, 136
  See also Human capital; Social
    capital
Caribbeans, 56
Cash flow, 48–49, 77, 81–82
Caucasians, 17, 18, 67
CDCs. *See* Community Development
  Corporations
CDLFs. *See* Community Development
  Loan Funds
CEP. *See* Community Enterprise
  Program
Check-cashing outlets, 52
Chicago, 6, 21–22n.15
Chinese, 61
Clubs, 53
Collateral, 71, 75, 123–24
College: and business success, 59–60
Communication skills, 72
Community, communities, 41, 99, 108,
  113–14n.12
  social capital in, 48, 60–62
Community Development
  Corporations (CDCs), 21n.15,
  152–53
Community Enterprise Program
  (CEP), 17, 88, 89, 160, 161
Constraints, 136
  on microcredit programs, 34–37,
    45–46n.5
  on microenterprise development,
    159–61
Context: socioeconomic and
  institutional, 37–41
Corner-store finance, 84–85
Corporation for Enterprise
  Development, 9
Costs, 138
  of microcredit programs, 125–27
  transaction, 23n.20, 97–98, 101
Credit, 71, 75
  and cash flow, 81–82
  delivery systems for, 142–43

and enterprise productivity, 27–28
  to groups, 86–87
  to individuals, 85–86
  informal, 84–85, 113–14n.12
  track record for, 58–59
Credit histories, 58–59, 71, 74, 75

Debt capacity, 77, 123, 124
Debt servicing, 77
Delaware, 7
Department of Health and Human
  Services, 7, 19–20n.3
Developing countries, 20n.4, 37–38,
  102

Economic Opportunity Loan (EOL)
  program, 12
Ecuador, 28
EDA. *See* Economic Development
  Administration
Education, 7, 56, 80n.10
  and enterprise development, 68–69
  and human capital, 59–60
  and loan repayment rates, 91,
    94–95, 106, 110, 136
Efficiency: internal and external,
  31–33
Enterprise Development Corporation,
  17, 160
Entrepreneurship, 79nn.4, 6, 116
  for poor business owners, 26–27
  capital and, 49–53
  communities and, 60–61
  constraints on, 50–56, 63–67, 136
  education and, 59–60
  lending criteria and, 58–59
  training in, 77–78
EOL. *See* Economic Opportunity Loan
  program
Equipment, 63, 67, 68
Ethnicity, 54, 55, 60–61, 79–80n.6

Family, 53, 61, 67, 74
FC. *See* First Chance
Fee structures, 129(table), 138–39

Financial intermediation, 138
  risk management and, 123–25
Financial services
  distribution of, 51–53
  markets and, 144–46
First Chance (FC), 17, 88, 89, 161
Florida, 7
Food sector, 71
Ford Foundation, 6, 21–22n.15
Friends, 53, 67, 74
Full Circle Fund, 6

Gardeners: Japanese American, 61–62
Garment contractors, 68
Gender, 55, 72–73
  and loan repayment rates, 90,
    96–97
Good Faith Fund, 6–7, 147, 156n.5
Grameen Bank, 3, 21n.10, 23n.21, 26,
    83
  lending strategy of, 86–87, 95
Grassroots organizations, 142
Group-based lending, 4, 6–7, 86–87,
    89, 106, 113nn.10, 11
  homogeneity of, 105, 162–63
  Neighborhood Entrepreneurship
    Program and, 17–18
  sanctions and, 98–99, 107–8
  social capital and, 124–25
Gujaratis, 55

Hispanics, 63, 67, 68, 71, 75, 160
Households, 50, 91, 124, 140
Human capital, 48, 75, 110
  building, 7, 69, 121–23
  constraints on, 59–60

IDAs. *See* Individual Development
    Accounts
Illinois, 7
Immigrants, 60, 79–80n.6,
    113–14n.12, 143
Income, 34, 77, 124, 114n.13, 136
  and financial service distribution,
    51–53

household, 27, 91
  microcredit programs and, 119–20
India, 38, 46n.8
Individual Development Accounts
    (IDAs), 48, 78–79n.2, 146,
    156n.3
Informal sector, 7
  credit, 84–85, 113–14n.12
  in the United States, 35–36, 119
Information, 52–53, 57–58, 61, 71
Inner cities, 138
  microcredit programs, 6, 12, 39–40
  banking and, 50–51
  redlining in, 56–57
  social capital in, 62–63, 125
Institute for Social and Economic
    Development, 147
Institutions, 34
  program evaluation of, 28–33
Interest rates, 86, 127, 129(table),
    138–39
  on small loans, 4, 21n.11
  and sustainability, 44–45n.4, 127,
    128
Intermediation, 14–15, 42–43
  financial, 123–25
  social, 117, 137–38
Iowa, 9
Italy, 62

Japanese Americans: as gardeners,
    61–62
Job creation, 120–21

Kinship, 61, 62, 98
Koreans, 55, 56, 61, 113n.12

Latinos/Latinas, 18, 63, 143
Latin America, 3
Lending agencies, 41, 43
  proximity of, 92, 95–96, 107, 111,
    137
Liability: mutual, 124–25
Lifestyle entrepreneurs, 36
LISTO, 143

Loan delivery systems, 82–83
Loans, 20n.5, 21n.9, 38, 56, 71, 74, 77,
     79n.5, 132n.2, 143
   administrative costs of, 39–40
   collateral substitutes and, 123–24
   criteria for, 57–59
   defaulting on, 41, 103–4, 107–8, 111
   delivery systems for, 82–83
   denial of, 118–19
   financial market and, 144–46
   to groups, 86–87
   for individual borrowers, 85–86
   losses on, 89–90, 112n.3, 113n.10
   microcredit programs, 88–89
   NEP, 122–23
   for poor businesses, 26–27
   repayment of, 81, 90–97
   and small-scale entrepreneurs, 2,
     3–4, 19n.1
   social networking and, 62, 67
   training and, 150–51
   WDA, 129–30
Loan repayment, 81, 107, 112n.1,
     136–37
   administration and, 130–31
   individual variables of, 90–97
   institutional variables of, 97–106
   performance, 161–63
Los Angeles, 21–22n.15, 51, 52(table),
     61, 74, 84–85, 143
Low-income households, 18, 19n.3,
     132n.1, 140

McArthur Foundation, 21–22n.15
Madagascar, 105
Maine, 7
Management skills, 54, 58–59, 63, 71,
     72, 80n.10
Market, marketing, 119
   and financial services, 144–46
   identification of, 59–60
   and microenterprise success, 13, 137
   and product, 69, 70
   and sales, 54–55, 79n.3
Massachusetts, 7

Michigan, 9
Microcredit programs, 4, 21–22nn.14,
     15, 18, 44n.2, 47, 135, 155–56
   in California, 16–18
   cash flow in, 81–82
   characteristics of, 88–89
   constraints on, 34–37, 45–46n.5
   costs of, 125–27
   entrepreneurship classes and, 77–78
   evaluation of, 27–28
   impacts of, 9–12
   institutional evaluation and, 28–33
   outreach, 117–21
   socioeconomic and institutional
     context of, 37–41
   strategies for, 12–13
   sustainability and, 42–43, 115–16
   in United States, 5–9
Microenterprise sector, 1–2, 117, 155–56
   constraints on, 34–37, 50–56,
     159–61
   development assistance, 26–27
   and poor, 139–40
   socioeconomics of, 64–66
   in United States, 7, 38–40
   viability in, 77–78
MicroFem, 121–22
Microloan Demonstration project
     (SBA), 130
Minnesota, 9
Mississippi, 9
Moneylenders, 84–85
Multiproduct strategy, 15

Neighborhood Enterprise Centers, 7
Neighborhood Entrepreneurship
     Program (NEP), 17–18, 88, 89,
     97, 104, 112n.4, 125, 160, 163
   loan repayment rates of, 99–101,
     107–9, 161
   training, 102–3, 122–23
Neighborhood Reinvestment
     Corporation, 7, 18
NEP. *See* Neighborhood
     Entrepreneurship Program

Networks, 8
    social, 60–61
New Hampshire, 7
New Institutional Economies (NIE),
    33–34
New Mexico, 7
New York, 7, 56, 61
NGOs. *See* Nongovernmental
    organizations
NIE. *See* New Institutional Economies
Nongovernmental organizations
    (NGOs), 26

Office of Refugee Resettlement, 7,
    127
Operational sustainability, 13, 14
Outreach, 29, 142–43
    breadth of, 117–19
    depth of, 119–21

Parsis, 55
Pawnbrokers, 52, 85
Peer pressure, 98–99
Permits, 37
Peru, 71
Pine Bluff (AK), 7
Policy formation, 16
Poor
    business development for, 26–27
    microenterprise and, 139–40, 141
    working, 102, 144
Portfolios
    expansion of, 118–19
    quality of, 130–31, 132n.2
Poverty, 7, 19–20n.3, 26, 62–63
Poverty level, 120
Product, 69
Productivity, 35
Profitability, profits, 71, 72, 76
Proximity: of lending agency, 92,
    95–96, 107, 111, 137
Public assistance, 7, 17
Putnam, Robert, 62

Reciprocity, 106, 108, 124, 142

Redlining, 56–57
Refugee Microenterprise Programs, 7
Returns on investment, 34
Revenues: generation of, 68, 76, 91
Risk assessment, 42
    and loan denial, 118–19
    and collateral, 123–24
    and social capital, 124–25
Risk management, 82, 83, 138

Safety nets, 39, 46n.7
Salaries: administrative, 128, 138
Sales, 54–55, 79n.3
San Antonio, 23n.19, 105
Sanctions, 46n.8
    for loan defaulting, 40, 41, 111
    and loan repayment, 98–99, 103–4,
        107–8, 109
Savings, 39, 113–14n.12, 145–46
SBA. *See* U.S. Small Business
    Administration
SDI. *See* Subsidy Dependence Index
Self Employed Women's Association
    (SEWA), 26
Self-employment, 7, 17, 18, 46n.6, 54,
    61–62, 144
Self-Employment Demonstration
    Project, 9
Self-sufficiency, 128, 132–33n.3
Self-sustainability, 29–30
SEWA. *See* Self Employed Women's
    Association
Sidewalk vendors, 55
Social capital, 40, 48, 142
    constraints on, 60–63, 75
    loan repayment and, 106, 110
    risk assessment and, 124–25
Social intermediation, 117, 137–38
Social justice, 143
Social policy, 128
Social standing, 99, 104
Social welfare, 8, 38–39, 46n.7
Socioeconomics
    and microcredit programs, 37–38
    of microenterprises, 64–66

South Shore Bank (Chicago), 21–22n.15
Sponsors, 15–16
Sri Lanka, 28
Street vendors, 35, 119
Subsidies, 128
Subsidy Dependence Index (SDI), 30
Sustainability, 44–45n.4, 115–16
   administrative factors of, 127–32
   enhancing, 152–54
   as evaluation factor, 29–30
   conditions for, 42–43
   social factors of, 117–27

Taxes, 37
Taxi drivers, 105
Technical assistance, 101–2, 149–50,
   153–54
Technology transfer, 6
Texas, 7
Third World, 16, 35, 113n.10, 119
   and loan delivery systems, 82–83
   loan repayment in, 108, 109
   risk assessment in, 123–24
   successful enterprises in, 14, 76–77
Training, 101–103, 110
   for microentrepreneurs, 7, 8
   MicroFem, 121–22
   NEP, 122–23
   as requirement, 147, 150–51
   WWB, 148–49
Transaction costs, 23n.20, 97–98, 101
Trust, 106, 108, 124

Unemployment Insurance Self-
   Employment Demonstration
   (UISED) program, 28

U.S. Small Business Administration
   (SBA), 130, 151

Vermont, 7

WBC. *See* Women's Business Centers
WDA. *See* Women's Development
   Association
Women
   Bangladeshi programs for, 27–28
   loan repayment rates of, 90, 97–98
   programs for, 18, 26
   training for, 121–22
Women in development, 5
Women's Business Centers (WBC),
   151
Women's Development Association
   (WDA), 18, 88, 112n.4, 125,
   161
   cost inefficiencies in, 126–27
   lending volume, 129–30
Women's Initiative for Self-
   Employment, 141
Women's Self Employment Project, 6,
   143
Women's World, 26
Women's World Banking (WWB),
   148–49
Working Capital program, 7, 23n.19,
   105, 120, 141, 156n.1
WWB. *See* Women's World Banking

Yaron, Jacob, 29
Yunus, Muhammad, 86–87

About the Author

Nitin Bhatt is practice leader and manager of Grant Thornton LLP's Management Consulting Services Practice in Los Angeles and former executive director of the University of Southern California's Business Expansion Network.

Bhatt has served as an advisor to numerous nonprofit organizations, government entities, and financial institutions on issues related to market and customer research, business strategy and planning, program design and evaluation, operational performance improvement, and project management. His work in the areas of entrepreneurship and economic development has been published in such journals as *Harvard Business Review, Economic Development Quarterly, Journal of Microfinance, Policy Studies Journal, World Development, International Journal of Public Administration,* and *International Journal of Urban and Regional Research.*

Bhatt holds an M.B.A. and a Ph.D. (with honors) from the University of Southern California.

About ICS

Founded in 1974, the Institute for Contemporary Studies (ICS) is a nonprofit, nonpartisan policy research institute.

To fulfill its mission to promote self-governing and entrepreneurial ways of life, ICS sponsors a variety of programs and publications on key issues including education, entrepreneurship, the environment, leadership, and social policy.

Through its imprint, ICS Press, the Institute publishes innovative and readable books that will further the understanding of these issues among scholars, policy makers, and the wider community of citizens. ICS Press books include the writing of eight Nobel laureates, and have been influential in setting the nation's policy agenda.

ICS programs seek to encourage the entrepreneurial spirit not only in this country but also around the world. They include the Institute for Self-Governance (ISG) and the International Center for Self-Governance (ICSG).